MOON

WITHDRAWN

This item is a gift
from the

Friends
of the
Danville Library

Friends of the Danville Library

LAS VEGAS

SCOTT SMITH

CONTENTS

Las Vegas

From the first glimpse of neon glowing in the middle of the empty desert, Las Vegas seduces the senses, indulges the appetites, and sparks the imagination.

Yosemite National Park

415 mi
8 hrs

Nevada
Utah

Utah
Arizona

LAS VEGAS

Lake Mead

Nevada
California

Grand Canyon National Park

280 mi
5 hrs

270 mi
5 hrs

LOS ANGELES

Joshua Tree National Park

LAS VEGAS

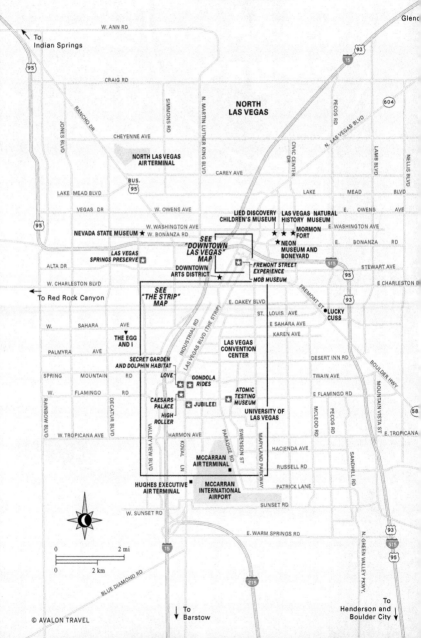

Glenc

To
Indian Springs

W. ANN RD

95

93

15

CRAIG RD

604

SIMMONS RD

N. MARTIN LUTHER KING BLVD

PECOS RD

N. LAS VEGAS BLVD

LAMB BLVD

NELLIS BLVD

RANCHO DR

JONES BLVD

NORTH
LAS VEGAS

CHEYENNE AVE

CIVIC CENTER DR

NORTH LAS VEGAS
AIR TERMINAL

CAREY AVE

BUS.
95

LAKE MEAD BLVD

LAKE   MEAD   BLVD

VEGAS DR

W. OWENS AVE

E. OWENS   AVE

95

LIED DISCOVERY
CHILDREN'S MUSEUM

LAS VEGAS NATURAL
HISTORY MUSEUM

W. WASHINGTON AVE

E. WASHINGTON AVE

NEVADA STATE MUSEUM ★

W. BONANZA RD

MORMON
★ ★ ★ FORT

E.   BONANZA   RD

SEE
"DOWNTOWN
LAS VEGAS"
MAP

★ NEON
MUSEUM AND
BONEYARD

LAS VEGAS
SPRINGS PRESERVE ✚

515

ALTA DR

DOWNTOWN
ARTS DISTRICT ★

✚

STEWART AVE

FREMONT STREET
EXPERIENCE

W. CHARLESTON BLVD

MOB MUSEUM

93

E CHARLESTON B

To Red Rock Canyon

SEE
"THE STRIP"
MAP

FREMONT ST

515

E. OAKEY BLVD

ST. LOUIS AVE

● LUCKY
CUSS

W.   SAHARA   AVE

E SAHARA AVE

▼
THE EGG
AND I

LAS VEGAS
CONVENTION
CENTER

KAREN AVE

PALMYRA   AVE

INDUSTRIAL RD

DESERT INN RD

BOULDER HWY

SPRING   MOUNTAIN   RD

SECRET GARDEN
AND DOLPHIN HABITAT

LOVE

GONDOLA
✚ RIDES

TWAIN AVE

W.   FLAMINGO   RD

✚

✚

MOUNTAIN VISTA ST

RAINBOW BLVD

DECATUR BLVD

LAS VEGAS BLVD ("THE STRIP")

CAESARS
PALACE

ATOMIC
TESTING
MUSEUM

E FLAMINGO RD

MCLEOD RD

PECOS RD

58

W. TROPICANA AVE

✚ JUBILEE!

HIGH
ROLLER

UNIVERSITY OF
LAS VEGAS

E. TROPICANA

HARMON AVE

VALLEY VIEW BLVD

KOVAL LN

PARADISE RD

SWENSON ST

MARYLAND PARKWAY

HACIENDA AVE

MCCARRAN
AIR TERMINAL

RUSSELL RD

SANDHILL RD

HUGHES EXECUTIVE
AIR TERMINAL ■

MCCARRAN
INTERNATIONAL
AIRPORT

PATRICK LANE

SUNSET RD

W. SUNSET RD

93

N. GREEN VALLEY PKWY.

515

95

E. WARM SPRINGS RD

0   2 mi

15

0   2 km

BLUE DIAMOND RD

215

© AVALON TRAVEL

↓ To
Barstow

To
Henderson and ↓
Boulder City ↓

Highlights

★ **Caesars Palace:** Caesars Palace carries on the Roman Empire's regality (and decadence) with over-the-top excess (page 21).

★ **Fremont Street Experience:** Part music video, part history lesson, the six-minute shows are a four-block-long, 12-million-diode, 550,000-watt burst of sensory overload (page 34).

★ **Gondola Rides:** Just like the real Grand Canal, only cleaner, The Venetian's waterway meanders along the Strip, with gondoliers providing the soundtrack (page 37).

★ **Secret Garden and Dolphin Habitat:** At the Mirage's twin habitats, the tigers, lions, and leopards can be seen playing impromptu games and the bottlenose dolphins never resist the spotlight (page 37).

★ **Mob Museum:** Explore what some old-timers still refer to as "the good old days," when wise guys ran the town, meting out their own brand of justice (page 36).

★ **High Roller:** The world's largest observation wheel overwhelms the senses with driving music, videos, and unmatched views of the Strip (page 38).

★ **Las Vegas Springs Preserve:** The city's birthplace, these natural springs now display the area's geological, anthropological, and cultural history along

with what may be its future: water-conserving "green" initiatives (page 39).

★ **Atomic Testing Museum:** Visit a fallout shelter and measure your body's radioactivity at this museum that traces the military, political, and cultural significance of the bomb (page 40).

★ *Jubilee!:* This show at Bally's pays tribute to one of Las Vegas's most enduring icons—the showgirl—in all her statuesque, sequined grandeur (page 42).

★ *LOVE:* Cirque du Soleil's magical mystery tour features artistry, acrobatics, and Beatles music in a surreal examination of the Fab Four's legacy (page 43).

An oasis of flashing marquees, feathered showgirls, chiming slot machines, and endless buffets, Las Vegas is a monument to fantasy.

With odds overwhelmingly favoring the house, jackpot dreams may be just that: dreams. The slim chance at fortune has lured vacationers into the southern Nevada desert ever since the Silver State legalized gambling in 1931. At first, the cowboy casinos that dotted downtown's Fremont Street were the center of the action, but they soon faced competition from a resort corridor blooming to the south on Highway 91. Los Angeles nightclub owner Billy Wilkerson dubbed it "The Strip," and together with Bugsy Siegel built the Flamingo, the first upscale alternative to frontier gambling halls. Their vision left a legacy that came to define Las Vegas hotel-casinos. Las Vegas has gone through many reinventions in the decades since—from city of sleaze to Mafia haven, family destination, and finally upscale resort town.

Today, each megaresort offers more to do than many small cities. Under one roof you can indulge in a five-star dinner, attend spectacular productions, dance until dawn with the beautiful people, and browse in designer boutiques. If there's still time, you can get a massage and ride a roller coaster too. The buffet, a fitting metaphor for this city with an abundance of everything, still rules in the hearts of many regulars and visitors, but an influx of celebrity chefs is turning the town into a one-stop marketplace of the world's top names in dining. Similarly, cutting-edge performers such as Blue Man Group and Cirque du Soleil have taken up residence.

So pack your stilettos, string bikini, money clip, and favorite hangover remedy and join the 35 million others who trek to Sin City every year to experience as many of the Seven Deadlies as they can cram into their vacation time. No

Best Hotels

★ **Harrah's:** It may seem middle-of-the-road, but its location puts it in the middle of the action (page 21).

★ **Wynn:** No castles, no pyramids. Opting for class over kitsch, substance over splash, the Wynn is a worthy heir to "Old Vegas" joints (page 18).

★ **Bellagio:** All the romance of Italy manifests through dancing fountains, lazy gondola rides, intimate bistros and—in case the spirit moves you—a wedding chapel (page 26).

★ **Cosmopolitan:** Part Museum of Modern Art, part *Cabaret* Kit Kat Klub, this center-Strip resort blends visual overload with sensuous swank (page 27).

★ **Aria:** The centerpiece of City Center makes no concessions to old-school Sin City, choosing an urban feel accentuated by marble, steel, glass, and silk (page 28).

★ **Mandalay Bay:** Let the conscientious staff and serene elegance of this end-of-the-Strip hotel take you away from Vegas's pounding hip-hop and clanging slot machines (page 32).

★ **Golden Nugget:** A Strip-style resort in the otherwise staid downtown district, the Nugget features a waterslide surrounded by a shark-filled aquarium (page 34).

★ **Mandarin Oriental:** Splurge for environmentally friendly luxury at this LEED-certified hotel (page 52).

one back home has to know you've succumbed to the city's siren song. After all, "What happens in Vegas . . . "

Getting to Las Vegas

From Los Angeles
Multilane highways ensure that the **270-mile, five-hour** drive from L.A. to Las Vegas is smooth, if not visually appealing. Even mild traffic can easily add an hour or more to your trip. Take **I-10 East** past Ontario to connect to **I-15 North.** Then continue 220 miles through Victorville, Barstow, and Baker before reaching Las Vegas.

Stopping in Calico
About two hours outside the L.A. environs, the restored boomtown of Calico is tourist-trappy but can make for a fun stop. It's just four miles off I-15 (take Exit 191 between Barstow and Yermo). The building exteriors at **Calico Ghost Town** (36600 Ghost Town Rd., Yermo, 800/86-CALICO—800/862-2542, daily 9am-5pm, $8, ages 6-15 $5, under age 6 free) are restored to their 1880s appearance, and they now house shops, restaurants, and attractions. The small museum, located in an original adobe building, contains original furnishings and gives a thorough overview of the town and its mining history. Pretend you're back in the Wild West: Pan for gold, ride a horse, tour the town by rail, tour a mine, and trick your eyes at the Mystery Shack (all cost extra).

The dining options stick to the ghost-town theme. At **Calico House Restaurant** (760/254-1970, Sun.-Fri. 8am-5pm, Sat. 8am-7:30pm, $10-20), the meat is smoked, the chili simmers all day, and Western art adorns the walls. **Lil's Saloon** (760/254-2610, Mon.-Fri. 11am-5pm, Sat.-Sun. 9am-5pm, $8-15) is full of Western ephemera—roulette wheels, a manual cash register, and gun collections. Munchies, including pizza, hot

Best Restaurants

★ **The Egg and I:** You can order something other than eggs—but given the name, why would you (page 55)?

★ **Mon Ami Gabi:** Order the baked gruyere and a baguette and channel your inner Hemingway for a traditional French Bistro experience (page 59).

★ **Culinary Dropout:** This creative gastropub takes its comfort food very seriously. The soft-pretzel fondue appetizer will have you dreaming of melted cheese (page 59).

★ **RM Seafood:** Soft lines and brushed metal accents evoke a glittering sea while the menu reflects chef Rich Moonen's advocacy of sustainable fishing practices (page 60).

★ **N9ne:** You *have* to get the steak, but make sure others in your party order the gnocchi and the lobster ravioli, so you can sneak bites from their plates (page 60).

★ **Rose. Rabbit. Lie:** Order six or eight small plates per couple, and let the sultry torch singers and rousing dancers play on as you nosh the night away (page 60).

★ **Le Thai:** The best of Las Vegas's impressive roster of Thai restaurants, Le Thai boasts playful interpretations of traditional Thai cuisine in a trendy yet unpretentious atmosphere (page 61).

★ **Phat Phrank's:** The no-frills presentation keeps the focus on the food: California- and New Mexico-inspired variations of traditional Mexican fare (page 62).

dogs, and giant pretzels, dominate the menu.

There's really no reason to visit the ghost town for more than a couple of hours, but overnight guests can bed down in a 4-person **cabin** (800/862-2542, www.sbcountyparks.com, $40), 6-person **mini-bunkhouse** ($100), or 12- to 20-person **bunkhouse** ($80). There are 265 **camping sites** ($30-35, seniors $25-30) for tents and with full and partial hookups.

From the Grand Canyon
From the West Rim

The good news is that the West Rim is the closest canyon point to Las Vegas—only about **120 miles,** or **2.5 hours,** even with the big detour south around the White Hills. The bad news is there's almost nothing to see along the way. If you parked and rode the shuttle from Meadview, take **Pierce Ferry Road** 39 miles down past Dolan Springs, Arizona, and pick up **US-93 North** for another 76 miles to Las Vegas.

From the South Rim

The South Rim is roughly **280 miles** or **5 hours** from Las Vegas. Take **US-180/AZ-64 South** for 55 miles to **Williams,** then **I-40 West** for 116 miles to **Kingman.** Here you'll connect with **US-93 North** for the final 100 miles of the journey to Las Vegas. Most summer weekends, you'll find the route crowded but manageable, unless there's an accident.

Stopping in Kingman

Proving ground for the manifest destiny of the United States, training ground for World War II heroes, and playground for the postwar middle class, Kingman preserves and proudly displays this heritage at several well-curated museums, such as the **Historic Route 66 Museum** and the **Mohave Museum of History and Arts.**

The best restaurant for miles in any direction is **Mattina's Ristorante Italiano** (318 E. Oak St., 928/753-7504, Tues.-Sat.

5pm-10pm, $13-25), where you can get perfectly prepared Italian food. It's difficult to pass up the lobster ravioli or the creamy fettuccini alfredo. Don't leave without trying the tiramisu or the key lime pie.

With a checkerboard floor, Formica tables, long counter, and comfort-food menu, **Rutherford's 66 Family Diner** (2011 E. Andy Devine Ave., 928/377-1660, Sun.-Thurs. 6am-9pm, Fri.-Sat. 6am-10pm, $8-16) is a 1950s diner straight out of Central Casting. Skillet breakfasts and steak and meatloaf sandwiches will have you waxing nostalgic.

There are several very affordable basic hotels on Andy Devine Avenue (Route 66) in Kingman's downtown area, some of them with retro road-trip neon signs and Route 66 themes. The Hollywood-themed **El Trovatore Motel** (1440 E. Andy Devine Ave., 928/692-6520, $56-76 d) boasts that Marilyn Monroe, James Dean, and Clark Gable all slept there. There are many chain hotels in town as well. One of only a handful of prewar motels left in town, the motel retains its art deco sign and architecture. Rooms, which command views of the Hualapai Mountains, are utilitarian, with king or queen beds, a microwave, and a fridge. Pets are welcome.

The small, affordable **Hill Top Motel** (1901 E. Andy Devine Ave., 928/753-2198, www.hilltopmotelaz.com, $47-55) beckons Route 66 road-trippers with a 1950s-era neon sign even cooler than El Trovator's. The motel maintains its nostalgic charms despite the addition of a swimming pool and in-room refrigerators and microwaves. Although it's located in the city center, the motel's guest rooms still overlook the mountains and are set back from the main streets, making use of block walls to deflect city noise.

From the North Rim

From the North Rim, it's a **5.5-hour, 280-mile** drive to Vegas. This route may appeal to canyon lovers, as it takes drivers through Utah's Zion National Park for another opportunity to view nature's handiwork with stone, wind, and water. Only attempt this route during good weather; AZ-67 is subject to closure early November-late May, and all facilities at the North Rim are closed mid-October-mid-May. From the North Rim, take **AZ-67 North** for 44 miles to **Jacob Lake**, and then head east on **US-89A** for 15 miles to **Fredonia**. Then take **AZ-389 West**, which becomes **UT-59 North**, for 55 miles to **Hurricane,** Utah. There pick up **UT-9 West** for 11 miles to **US-15 South.** It's then 125 miles to Las Vegas.

Stopping in Overton

Crossing into Nevada and approaching Glendale, look for the Overton exit. Twelve miles off the highway, Overton is a compact agricultural community whose downtown is strung along several blocks of NV-169, also known as Moapa Valley Boulevard and Main Street. Overton offers two strong lunch options. **Sugars Home Plate** (309 S. Moapa Valley Blvd., 702/397-8084, Tues.-Sun. 7am-9pm, $9-25) serves $7.50 bacon and eggs, $8-10 burgers, including the Sugar Burger, a cheeseburger with Polish sausage, and homemade pie. There's also a sports bar with bar-top video poker and sports memorabilia. Just a block away, **Inside Scoop** (395 S. Moapa Valley Blvd., 702/397-2055, Mon.-Sat. 11am-8pm, Sun. 11am-7pm, $10-25) has filling sandwiches and 30-plus ice cream flavors. The baked potatoes come with whatever toppings you can imagine. The **Plaza Motel** (207 Moapa Valley Blvd., 702/397-2414, $50-60) provides basic guest rooms and a jumping-off point for visits to Valley of Fire State Park.

From Yosemite

If there's any chance that the **Tioga Pass** is closed, which happens October-May, check with the **National Park Service** (209/372-0200, www.nps.gov/yose) for the latest **road conditions.** If the pass is open, you have your choice of two fairly direct routes to Las Vegas; both start by heading on **CA-120 East** through the pass to Mono Lake. If the pass is closed, prepare for a tedious **8- to 10-hour** trip through central California: **CA-41 South** to Fresno, **CA-99 South** to Bakersfield, and then **CA-58 East** to Barstow.

Via Tioga Pass: Nevada Route

The quickest route covers **415 miles,** with a typical driving time of **8 hours.** Follow **CA-120 East** to **Benton,** California (3 hours, 15 minutes). Take **US-6 East** to **Coaldale,** Nevada (35 minutes), where it shares the road with **US-95 South** for another 40 minutes to **Tonopah.** It's then a 210-mile, 3.5-hour straight shot on **US-95** to Las Vegas.

Stopping in Tonopah

Tonopah is a natural crossroads that rewards travelers with colorful mining history and one of the darkest starry skies in the country. Its restaurants specialize in old-fashioned American food and Mexican fare. The salsa seals the deal at **El Marquez** (348 N. Main St., 775/482-3885, Tues.-Sun. 11am-9pm, $12-25), where the enchiladas and cheesy chiles rellenos rule. If you're in a hurry but still jonesing for Mexican, hit the drive-through at **Cisco's Tacos** (702 N. Main St., 775/482-5022, daily 11am-8pm, $4-10), which has burgers, pizza, and ribs as well.

The owners have faithfully restored the **Mizpah Hotel** (100 Main St., 775/482-3030, www.mizpahhotel.net, $99-159), the "Grand Lady of Tonopah," with claw-foot tubs, wrought-iron bedsteads, and lots of carmine accents. You can dine on-site at the casual **Pittman Café** or the more formal **Jack Dempsey Room.** Next door, the guest rooms at **Jim Butler Motel** (100 S. Main St., 775/482-3577, www.jim-butlerinn.com, $70-115) are bright and inviting, with wood furniture and faux hearths. Some guest rooms have fridges and microwaves; all have free Wi-Fi.

Stretch Your Legs

Ever wonder what it would be like to live upside down? Satisfy your curiosity at the Upside-Down House (Yosemite-Las Vegas Drive, corner of 1st Ave. and Matley Ave., Lee Vining, 760/547-6461, www.monobasinhs.org, Thurs.-Mon. 10am-4pm, Sun. noon-4pm, $2), just a block off US-395 outside of Yosemite National Park. Inspired by the children's stories "Upside Down Land" and "The Upsidedownians," the small wooden cabin features a bed, a rug, and furniture on the ceiling.

The infamous Area 51 is the focus of conspiracy theories about UFOs. Capitalizing on its location just south of the secret military installation, the Area 51

Alien Travel Center (Yosemite-Las Vegas Drive, 2711 E. US-95, Amargosa Valley, 775/372-5678) sells all sorts of extraterrestrial-influenced merchandise. Painted fluorescent yellow, it's hard to miss. (This being, Nevada, there's also a brothel out back.)

Last Stop Arizona (Yosemite-Las Vegas Drive, 20606 N. US-93, White Hills, 928/767-4911, www.arizonalaststop.com, gift store daily 6:30am-8pm, restaurant daily 7am-6pm) also celebrates life on other planets. Pose for a photo in an alien cutout display and fill up your tank with "Uranus" gas. There's also a diner and a quirky gift shop, which doubles as a source of Powerball lottery tickets.

Via Tioga Pass: California Route

Only a few miles farther but 45 minutes longer, an arguably more scenic route—taking US-395 South from CA-120, rather than continuing on to US-6—traverses Mammoth Lakes, Bishop, and Lone Pine, California, and includes views of Mount Whitney and the possibility of an overnight stay at Death Valley National Park. Follow CA-120 East to US-395 South. At Lone Pine, California, take CA-136 East. This becomes CA-190 West, which winds through Death Valley. A left turn onto the Daylight Pass Road leads to the Nevada border and NV-374 North just before Beatty. From Beatty, US-95 South leads 117 miles to Las Vegas.

Stopping in Beatty

Once a center of Nevada mining, Beatty is a microcosm of Western history, serving at various times as a Shoshone settlement, a ranching center, and a railway hub.

The Harleys and pickups in the parking lot are the first clue that the Sourdough Saloon and Restaurant (106 W. Main St., 775/553-2266, daily noon-9pm, $10-20) features pizza and bar snacks to accompany fermented grain

beverages. While the food isn't memorable, the friendly folks and the desert dive-bar experience certainly are. The clientele is well-behaved, give or take the occasional late weekend night, but there's also a family-friendly back room for parents who don't want to take any chances.

The laundry room and small pool and spa at Death Valley Inn (651 US-95 S., 775/553-9400, $75-95) are welcome amenities greeting road-weary travelers. There's also a 39-space RV park—all pull-throughs with 50-amp hookups. Originally serving defense contractor employees at the Nevada Test Site and Area 51, the Atomic Inn (350 S. 1st St., 775/553-2250, $50-70) has standard guest rooms, with lots of golds and honey-blond wood furniture and paneling.

Bypassing Tioga Pass

If Tioga Pass is closed—ugh. The only way to Las Vegas is an ugly 8- to 10-hour, 500-mile ordeal. Take CA-41 South 95 miles to Fresno (2.5 hours), and then follow CA-99 South to Bakersfield (1 hour 45 minutes). Continue on CA-58 East to Barstow (2 hours 15 minutes) before catching US-95 North to Las Vegas (2.5 hours).

Stopping in Bakersfield

While far from a tourist destination, Bakersfield is at least a diversion on the otherwise dreary winter Yosemite-Las Vegas route.

Skip the chains and treat yourself to lodgings with character. With eight stories of Spanish colonial revival architecture, the **Padre Hotel** (1702 18th St., 888/443-3387, $129-199), has been faithfully restored to its 1930s grandeur. But the rooms are strictly 21st century, with sleek furniture and plush textiles. Kick off your shoes, soak in a chromatherapy spa tub, then snuggle into a fine down comforter to guarantee a fine night's rest. Or bust a move in the hotel's fifth-floor Prospect Lounge.

A few blocks west, the guest rooms at **Hotel Rosedale** (2400 Camino Del Rio Court, 661/327-0681, $79-149) lure guests with their springy umber, burnt orange, and green decor. The oversize pool is surrounded by plenty of shade and shrubbery. A small playground will keep little tykes busy, while an arcade ensures older children don't lose their video-game dexterity while on vacation.

You wouldn't think cabbage could form the basis for a hearty and satisfying meal. But you'd be proven wrong if you visit **Bit of Germany** (1901 Flower St., 661/325-8874, 11am-2pm and Mon.-Sat. 5pm-8pm, $10-15). Stuffed, rolled or shredded into a salad, it's "head" and shoulders above any other German joint in town. They offer a solid selection of Bavarian beers, and their wurst (brat, knack, and weiss) is among the best.

More highbrow, **Uricchio's Trattoria** (1400 17th St., 661/326-8870, Mon.-Thurs. 11am-2pm and 5pm-9pm, Fri. 11am-2pm and 5pm-10pm, Sat. 5pm-10pm, $15-30) serves the best chicken *piccata;* seafood fans can't go wrong with the diver scallops or orange roughy almandine.

By Air and Bus
Air
More than 900 planes arrive or depart **McCarran International Airport** (LAS, 5757 Wayne Newton Blvd., 702/261-5211, www.mccarran.com) every day, making it the sixth busiest in the country and 19th in the world. Terminal 1 hosts domestic flights, while Terminal 3 has domestic and international flights.

About 40 percent of the runway traffic at McCarran belongs to **Southwest Airlines,** by far the largest carrier serving Las Vegas. Other major players include **United, Delta, American,** and **Spirit.** The number of airlines keeps fares competitive. Given that Las Vegas is one of the world's top tourist destinations, it's best to make your reservations as early as possible. Last-minute deals are few and far between, and you'll pay through the nose to fly to Vegas on a whim.

United and Virgin offer roundtrip **flights from San Francisco** for as low as $170-220, when booked well in advance. Flight time is 1.5 hours. **Flights from Los Angeles** (LAX or Long Beach) are available on Spirit and JetBlue for as low as $175-200, even at the last minute. Virgin, Delta, and United will do the job for $230 or so. Flight time is 70 minutes.

McCarran Airport provides easy transfers to the Las Vegas Strip using **shuttle vans, buses,** and **rental cars.** Limousines are available curbside for larger groups. A **taxi ride** from the airport to the Strip (15 minutes) or downtown (20 minutes) runs no more than $25. A $2 surcharge is assessed for pickups from the airport, and there is a $3 credit card processing fee. It's cheaper and often faster to take the surface streets from the airport to your destination rather than the freeway, which is several miles longer.

Bus
Las Vegas City Area Transit **buses** serve the airport. **Route 108** runs north from McCarran on Swenson Street, and the closest it comes to Las Vegas Boulevard is the corner of Paradise Road and West Sahara Avenue, but you can connect with the **Las Vegas monorail** at several

stops. If you're headed downtown, stay on the bus to the end of its 45-minute line. Alternately, grab the Route 109 bus, which runs east of the 108 up Maryland Parkway. To get to the Strip, you have to transfer at the large cross streets onto westbound buses that cross the Strip. The northbound 109 stops at Tropicana Avenue, Flamingo Road, Desert Inn Road, Sahara Avenue, and Charleston Boulevard. Route 109 also ends up at the Downtown Transportation Center. Bus fare is $2, with passes of varying duration available. Travel time is 20 to 35 minutes, depending on how far north your hotel is located.

Gray Line is one of several companies that will ferry you via airport shuttle to your Strip ($12 round-trip) or downtown ($16 round-trip) hotel. All have ticket kiosks inside the terminals, most near the baggage claim. These shuttles run continuously, leaving about every 15 minutes. You don't need reservations from the airport, but you will need reservations from your hotel to return to the airport.

The **Greyhound Depot** (200 S. Main St., 702/383-9792) is on the south side of the Plaza Hotel. Buses arrive and depart frequently throughout the day and night to and from all points in North America, and they are a reasonable alternative to driving or flying.

Five of six buses originating at the **San Francisco station** (200 Folsom St., 415/495-1569) arrive in Las Vegas each day after 12- to 17-hour slogs through California and Nevada. Tickets can be had for as little as $27, if booked well in advance, purchased online and without the possibility of a refund. Last-minute tickets with same stipulations are $50-60, and standard rates are 25 to 50 percent higher.

Eight to ten Greyhounds arrive from the **Los Angeles terminal** (1716 E. 7th Street, 213/629-8401) each day. Travel time can be as little as five hours, with a single stop in either San Bernardino or Barstow. Rates are a reasonable $15-30,

with some as low as $6 when purchased well ahead of time.

Megabus (Patsaouras Transit Plaza, One Gateway Plaza, Los Angeles, 877/462-6342) runs four buses a day from Los Angeles, for $28-30 pp. It delivers passengers to the Regional Transportation Center's South Strip Transfer Terminal. Those heading to the Strip or downtown can catch the "Deuce" double-decker bus at Bay 14. It runs 24 hours a day, seven days a week, and the next one will be there in less than 15 minutes.

Orientation

Las Vegas Boulevard South—better known as The Strip—is the city's focal point, with 15 of the 20 largest hotels in the world lining a four-mile north-south stretch between Tropicana and Sahara Avenues. Running parallel to Interstate 15, this is what most folks think of when someone says "Vegas."

The **Lower Strip**—roughly between the "Welcome to Fabulous Las Vegas" sign and Harmon Avenue—is a living city timeline. The Tropicana is here, providing a link to the mobbed-up city of the 1960s and 1970s. Camelot-themed Excalibur, completed in 1990, and the Egyptian-inspired Luxor, which opened in 1993, serve as prime examples from the city's hesitant foray into becoming a "family" destination in the early 1990s. Across from the Tropicana, the MGM Grand opened in 1993 as a salute to *The Wizard of Oz*. One of Vegas's first destination hotels, it was also one of the first to abandon the family market, bulldozing the adjacent theme park in favor up upscale condos. City Center puts the mega in mega-resort—condos, boutique hotels, trendy shopping, a huge casino, and a sprawling dining and entertainment district—that cemented the city's biggest-is-best trend. The Lower Strip seems made for budget-conscious families. Rooms are often cheaper than mid-Strip. There are plenty of kid-friendly attractions (even a roller coaster).

The **Center Strip** is between Harmon Avenue and Spring Mountain Road. If the Lower Strip is a longitudinal study, the Center Strip is a cross section of the varied experiences today's visitors can choose. The well-heeled can sip martinis at Caesars Palace; the flat-stomached can flaunt it at the Cosmopolitan's Marquee Day Club; and the rubber-necked can marvel at the Eiffel Tower, fountains, volcanoes, and whimsical floral displays. Center Strip and its patrons share Type-A personalities. The casinos are packed tight, and though the sidewalks can become masses of humanity on weekend nights, all the temptations are within walking distance.

Ranging from Spring Mountain Road to the Stratosphere, the **Upper Strip** received a shot of much-needed exuberance with opening of the opulent SLS resort on the site of the old Sahara Hotel. The north end of the Strip now has something for everyone, Along with SLS's throwback swagger, visitors can opt for the world-class art, champagne pedicures, and celebrity chef creations at Wynn and Encore or the midway games, stand-up comedy, and friendly rates at old standbys such as Circus Circus, Westgate, and Riviera.

Major east-west thoroughfares include Tropicana Avenue, Harmon Avenue, Flamingo Road, Spring Mountain Road, Desert Inn Road, and Sahara Avenue. Koval Lane and Paradise Road parallel the Strip to the east, while Frank Sinatra Drive does likewise to the west, giving a tour of the loading docks and employee parking lots of some of the world's most famous resorts.

Interstate 15 also mirrors the Strip to the east, as both continue north-northeast through the **Downtown** and its casino district. Main Street juts due south at Charleston Boulevard and joins Las Vegas Boulevard at the Stratosphere. The Strip and I-15 continue parallel southeast and south out of town.

Casinos

Upper Strip
Stratosphere Casino, Hotel, and Tower

Restaurants: Top of the World, McCalls, The Buffet, Roxy's Diner, Fellini's Ristorante Italiano, Level 8 Pool Café, Tower Pizzeria, Sandwich Carvery 108, Starbucks
Entertainment: Frankie Moreno, *Pin Up*
Attractions: Observation Deck, Top of the Tower thrill rides
Nightlife: Level 107 Lounge, Images Lounge, C Bar, McCall's Heartland Grill Bar, Airbar, Level 8 Pool Bar, Race & Sportsbook Bar

It's altitude with attitude at this 1,149-foot-tall exclamation point on the north end of the Strip. Depending on how nitpicky you want to be, the **Stratosphere Tower** (200 Las Vegas Blvd. S., 702/380-7777 or 800/99-TOWER—800/998-6937, $69-200 d) is either the largest *building* west of Chicago or the largest *tower* west of St. Louis. Entrepreneur, politician, and professional poker player Bob Stupak opened the Stratosphere in 1996 as a marked improvement over his dark and dive-y Vegas World Casino. Daredevils will delight in the vertigo-inducing thrill rides on the tower's observation deck. The more faint-of-heart may want to steer clear not only of the rides but also the resort's double-decker elevators that launch guests to the top of the tower at 1,400 feet per minute. But even agoraphobes should conquer their fears long enough to enjoy the views from the restaurant and bars more than 100 floors up, and the **Chapel in the Clouds** can ensure a heavenly beginning to married life.

If the thrill rides on the observation deck aren't your style, get a rush of gambling action on the nearly 100,000-square-foot ground-floor casino, two swimming pools (one where you can go topless), and a dozen bars and restaurants more your speed.

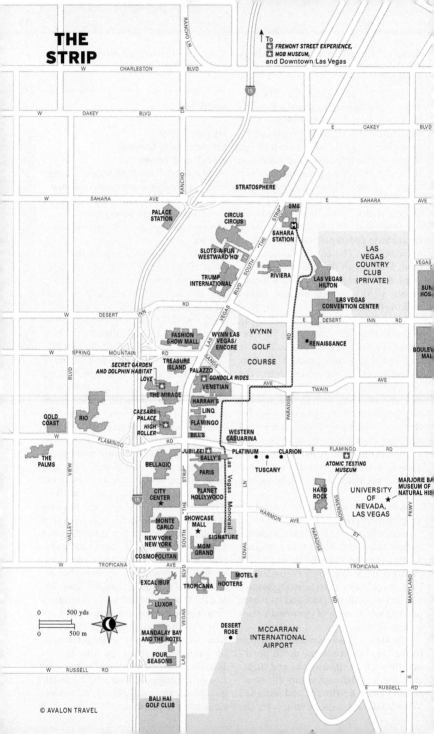

THE STRIP

To
⭐ FREMONT STREET EXPERIENCE,
⭐ MOB MUSEUM,
and Downtown Las Vegas

W CHARLESTON BLVD

W OAKEY BLVD
E OAKEY BLVD

STRATOSPHERE

W SAHARA AVE
E SAHARA AVE

SMS

PALACE STATION

CIRCUS CIRCUS

Ⓜ SAHARA STATION

LAS VEGAS COUNTRY CLUB (PRIVATE)

VEGAS

SLOTS-A-FUN WESTWARD HO!

RIVIERA

LAS VEGAS HILTON

SUN HOS

W DESERT INN RD

TRUMP INTERNATIONAL

LAS VEGAS CONVENTION CENTER

E DESERT INN RD

W SPRING MOUNTAIN RD

FASHION SHOW MALL

WYNN LAS VEGAS/ENCORE

WYNN GOLF COURSE

• RENAISSANCE

BOULEVARD MAL

TREASURE ISLAND

SECRET GARDEN AND DOLPHIN HABITAT

LOVE

PALAZZO

⭐ GONDOLA RIDES

☆ THE MIRAGE

VENETIAN

TWAIN

GOLD COAST

RIO

CAESARS PALACE

HARRAH'S

LINQ

FLAMINGO

HIGH ROLLER

BILL'S

WESTERN CASUARINA

W FLAMINGO RD
E FLAMINGO RD

THE PALMS

JUBILEE! ⭐

BALLY'S

PLATINUM

CLARION

ATOMIC TESTING MUSEUM

PARIS

TUSCANY

BELLAGIO

MARJORIE BA MUSEUM OF NATURAL HIS

PLANET HOLLYWOOD

HARD ROCK

UNIVERSITY OF NEVADA, LAS VEGAS ★

CITY CENTER ★

HARMON AVE

MONTE CARLO

SHOWCASE MALL ★

NEW YORK NEW YORK

SIGNATURE

MGM GRAND

COSMOPOLITAN

W TROPICANA AVE
E TROPICANA AVE

MOTEL 6

EXCALIBUR

TROPICANA

HOOTERS

LUXOR

DESERT ROSE •

McCARRAN INTERNATIONAL AIRPORT

0   500 yds
0   500 m

MANDALAY BAY AND THE HOTEL

FOUR SEASONS

W RUSSELL RD
E RUSSELL RD

BALI HAI GOLF CLUB

© AVALON TRAVEL

Two Days in Las Vegas

Day 1

Pick a hotel based on your taste and budget. May we suggest **Harrah's**? It gets a bad rap as a stodgy, but it's smack in the middle of the action, across from the Mirage and Caesars Palace and within walking distance of The Venetian and The Palazzo.

Get your gambling fix for a few hours before hoofing it across the Strip for brunch at the Mirage's **Cravings Buffet.** It operates on a familiar theory, with separate stations highlighting different cuisines. After the gorge-fest, you'll be ready for a nap, and you'll need it. This is Vegas; no early nights for you!

Couples should start the evening off with a romantic dinner at Paris's **Mon Ami Gabi**. For a more modest meal, a mustardy pastrami sandwich at The Mirage's **Carnegie Deli** hits the spot. If you only have time for one show, make it *LOVE* at The Mirage. The show is a loose biography of the Beatles' creative journey, told by tumblers, roller-skaters, clowns, and the characters from John, Paul, George, and Ringo's songs—Eleanor Rigby, Lucy in the Sky, Sgt. Pepper, and others.

Day 2

Celebrate the kitsch and class of vintage Vegas. Head downtown to stock up on Elvis sideburns and Sammy Davis Jr. sunglasses before loading up on eggs benedict and 1970s flair at the **Peppermill Restaurant and Fireside Lounge**. While it's daylight, make your way to the **Neon Museum and Boneyard**, the final resting place of some of Las Vegas's iconic signage. And while you're in the neighborhood, witness the rise and fall of the Mafia in Las Vegas at the **Mob Museum**.

Back at the hotel, change into your glad rags and beat it over to the Flamingo. Order up a neat bourbon and watch Sinatra try to make it through a rendition of "Luck Be a Lady" while Dino, Joey, and Sammy heckle and cut up from the wings in Sandy Hackett's *The Rat Pack Is Back*. Then get out there and gamble into the wee hours! For a chance to rub elbows with celebrities, head over to **Lavo** at The Palazzo or **Tao** at The Venetian. Kim and Kanye are regular visitors.

Frankie Moreno takes the Stratosphere Theater stage (Wed.-Sun. 8pm, $44), with song stylings and audience patter reminiscent of Sinatra and Michael Bublé. Backed by a swingin' 10-piece band, Moreno belts out the standards and an eclectic collection of original material. It's one of the most underrated and underpriced shows in town. The showroom also hosts *Pin Up* (Thurs.-Mon. 10:30pm, $55), a cheeky (all four cheeks), musical examination of a year in the life of sexy, but not raunchy, vixens. Picture a soft-R-rated video of Neil Sedaka's *Calendar Girl*.

Roxy's Diner (daily 24 hours, $12-15) is a trip back to the malt shop for comfort food and singing waitresses.

SLS

Restaurants: Katsuya, Bazaar Meat, Cleo, Ku Noodle, Umami Burger, 800 Degrees, Griddle Café, SLS Buffet, The Perq

Nightlife: Sayers Club, Foxtail, Life, Shot Bar, Monkey Bar, Center Bar

Located on the site of the legendary Sahara Casino, **SLS** (2535 Las Vegas Blvd. S., 855/761-7757, $155-245 d) targets go the swanky sophisticate market. Its management team, SBE Entertainment Group, built its reputation with exclusive restaurants, nightclubs, and boutique hotels in the ritziest destinations in the country—Beverly Hills, South Beach, and Manhattan. SLS incorporates those proven nightspot and restaurant brands, channeling Rat Pack cool through a modern lens to become a major player in Vegas.

Three towers offer standard rooms of 325 to 435 square feet. All boast 55-inch televisions, soft pastel accents, and 300-thread-count sheets atop BeautyRest mattresses. The all-suite Lux Tower attracts the resort visitors features with peek-a-boo showers and other amenities. World Tower rooms take aim at business travelers, with extra seating areas and infinity sinks. Story is for the urban crowd, featuring big beds as center points for socialization.

Chef Jose Andres doesn't want guests at **Bazaar Meat** (Sun.-Thurs. 5:30pm-10:30pm, Fri.-Sat. 5:30pm-midnight, $60-100) ordering huge T-bones or leg of lamb or inch-thick tuna steaks. He wants you to try them all. His Spanish-influenced meat-centric dishes are meant to be shared with everyone in your party. The restaurant's decor reinforces that aim, with long communal tables, open cooking stations, and a small gaming area.

Sayers Club (Thurs.-Sun. 8pm-2pm) bills itself as a live-music venue, but with lots of open space and an industrial-warehouse feel, it's a natural environment for DJs. The go-go cages, platforms, and poles seem imported en masse from L.A.'s Hollywood Boulevard.

Wynn Las Vegas/Encore

Restaurants: Andreas, Bartolotta Ristorante di Mare, Botero, The Country Club, Lakeside Seafood, Mizumi, Sinatra, SW Steakhouse, Tableau, Wing Lei, The Buffet, Drugstore Café, La Cave, Red 8, Society Café, Terrace Pointe Café, Wazuzu, Zoozacrackers
Entertainment: Le Rêve, Michael Monge
Attractions: Lake of Dreams, Wynn Golf Course, Penske Wynn Ferrari
Nightlife: XS, Surrender, Encore Beach Club, Tryst

An eponymous monument to indulgence, ★ **Wynn** (3131 Las Vegas Blvd. S., 702/770-7000 or 888/320-9966, $259-500 d) marked the $2.5 billion return of Steve Wynn, "the man who made Las Vegas," to the Strip in 2005. Wynn invites fellow multimillionaires to wallow in the good life and the hoi polloi to sample a taste of how the other half lives: Gaze at Wynn's art, one of the best and most valuable private collections in the world, or drool over the horsepower at **Penske Wynn Ferrari dealership** Wynn partly owns. If you're not in the market for an $800,000 ride, logo T-shirts, coffee mugs, and key chains are also available.

Never one to rest on his laurels, Wynn opened the appropriately named Encore Tower next door in 2008. Red must be his favorite color, because the casino area is awash in it. The twins' opulence is matched by the resort's Tom Fazio-designed golf course, open to hotel guests only, of course. Although guests come to explore the privileges of wealth, they can also experience the wonders of nature without the inconvenience of bugs and dirt. Lush plants, waterfalls, lakes, and mountains dominate the pristine landscape.

In addition to the gourmet offerings, don't miss the dim sum at **Red 8 Asian Bistro** (Sun.-Thurs. 11:30am-11pm, Fri.-Sat. 11:30am-1am, $25-35). **Bartolotta** (daily 5:30pm-10pm, $40-60) works as hard on creating a sense of the Mediterranean seaside as it does on its cuisine. Sample the fish flown in daily from Italian coastal waters while seated around a placid lagoon. The à la carte menu and especially the tasting menus are quite dear, but the appetizers will give you a sense of Italy for about $25.

Wynn-Encore's formal sophistication belies its location on the site of the old Desert Inn with the unself-conscious swagger Frank, Dino, and Sammy brought to the joint. Both towers boast some of the biggest guest rooms and suites on the Strip, with the usual although better-quality amenities and a few extra touches, like remote-controlled drapes, lights, and air-conditioning. Wynn's guest rooms are appointed in wheat, honey, and other creatively named shades of beige. Encore is more colorful, with the color scheme running toward dark chocolate and cream.

Center Strip
The Venetian

Restaurants: AquaKnox, B&B Ristorante, Bouchon, Canaletto, db Brasserie, Delmonico Steakhouse, Postrio, Tau, Zeffirino, B&B Burger &Beer, Buddy V's Ristorante, Café Presse, Cañonita, Canyon Ranch Café, Carlo's Bakery, Casanova, Grand Lux Café, Lobster ME, Noodle Asia, Otto Enoteca Pizzeria, Public House, Rockhouse, Tintoretto Restaurant & Bakery, Trattoria Reggiano

Entertainment: *Georgia on My Mind, Lipshtick, Rock of Ages, Human Nature*

Attractions: Madame Tussauds Las Vegas, Gondola Rides, Streetmosphere

Nightlife: Tao, Tao Beach, Bellini Bar, Rockhouse, Bourbon Room, V Bar

While Caesars Palace bears little resemblance to the realities of ancient Rome and Luxor doesn't really replicate the land of the pharaohs, **The Venetian** (3355 Las Vegas Blvd. S., 702/414-1000 or 866/659-9643, $210-370 d) comes pretty close to capturing the elegance of Venice. An elaborate faux-Renaissance ceiling fresco greets visitors in the hotel lobby, and the sensual treats just keep coming. A life-size streetscape with replicas of the Bridge of Sighs, Doge's Palace, the Grand Canal, and other treasures give the impression that the best of the Queen of the Adriatic has been transplanted in toto. Tranquil rides in authentic gondolas with serenading pilots are perfect for relaxing after a hectic session in the 120,000-square-foot casino. Canal-side, buskers entertain the guests in the **Streetmosphere** (various times and locations daily, free), and the **Grand Canal Shoppes** (Sun.-Thurs. 10am-11pm, Fri.-Sat. 10am-midnight) entice strollers, window shoppers, and serious spenders along winding streetscapes. Don't miss the magicians at Houdini's Magic Shop, and treat yourself at Barney's New York.

After you've shopped till you're ready to drop, **Madame Tussauds Interactive Wax Museum** (daily 10am-10pm, adults $30, over age 59 $18, ages 4-12 $20, under age 4 free) invites stargazers for hands-on experiences with their favorite entertainers and sports stars. Then you can dance the night away at **Tao** (nightclub Thurs.-Sat. 10pm-5am, lounge Sun.-Wed. 5pm-midnight, Thurs.-Sat. 5pm-1am).

Fine dining options abound, but for a change, **Trattorio Reggiano** (daily 10am-midnight, $20-30) offers pizza and pasta dishes in a bistro setting. The Venetian spares no expense in the hotel department. Its 4,027 suites are tastefully appointed with Italian (of course) marble, and at 700 square feet, they're big. They include roomy bedrooms with two queen beds and comfy sitting rooms.

The Palazzo

Restaurants: Carnevino, Cut, LAVO, Morels French Steakhouse & Bistro, Table 10, SushiSamba, Café Presse, Canyon Ranch Grill, Dal Toro Ristorante, Espressamente Illy, Grand Lux Café, Grimaldi's, I Love Burgers, JuiceFarm, Legasse's Stadium, Zine Noodles Dim Sum

Entertainment: *Panda*

Attractions: Grand Canal Shoppes, Atrium Waterfall

Nightlife: Laguna Champagne Bar, Double Helix, LAVO Lounge, Zebra Lounge, Fusion Latin Mixology Bar, The Lounge at SushiSamba

The lobby at **The Palazzo** (3325 Las Vegas Blvd. S., 702/607-7777 or 866/263-3001, $210-370 d), The Venetian's sister property next door, is bathed in natural light from an 80-foot domed skylight focused on a faux-ice sculpture, bronze columns and lush landscaping. Motel 6 this ain't. Half of the 100,000-square-foot casino is smoke-free, part of The Palazzo's efforts in achieving energy efficiency and environmentally friendly design.

The production show at Palazzo is heavy on kung fu and pandas, but the resemblance to a certain DreamWorks animated film stops there. *Panda* (Fri.-Tues. 7:30pm, $68-158) tells of LongLong's quest to rescue his kidnapped beloved and subdue the vulture villain. Told through expressive performance artists, acrobats, and martial arts, the show

makes it easy to suspend your disbelief just long enough for the happy ending.

Las Vegas has carved out a niche as a bachelorette party central, and **Lavo** (Fri.-Sat. 6pm-1am) is well-positioned to treat the bride-to-be and her entourage in the style to which they hope to become accustomed. With decor reminiscent of a library, Lavo pours top-shelf booze amid subdued lighting, first editions, and burnished leather.

The Palazzo is a gourmand's dream, with a handful of four-star establishments. A refreshing counterpoint to dark, woody steakhouses that seem to spring up in Vegas, **Carnevino** (daily noon-midnight, $40-70) is light and bright, with snootiness kept to a minimum. That does not mean Chef Mario Batali skimps on quality. He selects the best cuts, then refrains from overwhelming them in preparation. Salt, pepper, rosemary, and a little butter are all that's required.

Accommodations are all suites, with roman tubs, sunken living rooms, and sumptuous beds that would make it tough to leave the room if not for the lure of the Strip.

The Mirage

Restaurants: Tom Colicchio's Heritage Steak, FIN, Morimoto, Stack, Portofino, Samba Brazilian Steakhouse, BLT Burger, California Pizza Kitchen, Cravings Buffet, Carnegie Delicatessen, Paradise Café, Pantry, Blizz Frozen Yogurt, The Roasted Bean, Starbucks

Entertainment: The Beatles *LOVE*, Terry Fator Boys II Men, Aces of Comedy

Attractions: Secret Garden and Dolphin Habitat, Aquarium, Mirage volcano, Atrium

Nightlife: 1 Oak, Revolution Lounge, Rhumbar, High Limit Lounge, The Sports Bar, Dolphin Bar, Bare Pool Lounge, Lobby Bar, Stack Lounge

While grand and attention-grabbing, **The Mirage** (3400 Las Vegas Blvd. S.,

---

From top to bottom: The Beatles *LOVE* carries on the spirit of the Fab Four; The Mirage's Dolphin Habitat; *Million Dollar Quartet* at Harrah's.

702/791-7111 or 800/627-6667, $155-300 d) was the first understated megaresort, starting a trend that signifies Las Vegas's return to mature pursuits. This Bali Ha'i-themed paradise lets guests bask in the wonders of nature alongside the sophistication and pampering of resort life. More an oasis than a mirage, the hotel greets visitors with exotic bamboo, orchids, banana trees, secluded grottoes, and peaceful lagoons. Dolphins, white tigers, stingrays, sharks, and a volcano provide livelier sights.

1 Oak (Tues. and Fri.-Sat. 10:30am-4am) has two separate rooms with bars and DJs and crowded dance floors. With dark walls and no lighting, 1 Oak makes no excuses for providing a sinful, sexy venue for the beautiful people to congregate.

The Mirage commands performances by the world's top headliners, but **The Beatles *LOVE*** packs 'em in every night. It's a celebration of the Fab Four's music, but even more an exploration of classic Beatles tunes come to life. Acrobats, roller-skaters, clowns, and specialty acts conjure up the Walrus, Nowhere Men, and Lovely Rita.

Since a 2008 renovation, the Mirage's guest rooms have jettisoned the South Pacific theme in favor of tasteful appointments and some of the most comfortable beds in town. The facelift gave Mirage guest rooms a modern and relaxing feel in browns, blacks, and splashes of tangerine, mauve, and ruby.

Harrah's

Restaurants: Ruth's Chris Steak House, KGB: Kerry's Gourmet Burgers, Flavors, the Buffet, Oyster Bar, Ice Pan, Starbucks, Toby Keith's I Love This Bar & Grill
Entertainment: *Million Dollar Quartet*, The Improv Comedy Club, Mac King Comedy Show, Defending the Caveman
Nightlife: Carnaval Court, Numb Bar, Piano Bar
Seemingly unwilling to engage in the one-upmanship of its neighbors, ★ **Harrah's** (3475 Las Vegas Blvd. S., 800/898-8651, $50-160 d) has been content instead to carve out a niche as a middle-of-the-action, middle-of-the-road, middle-of-the-price-scale option. But with the Linq pedestrian thoroughfare with bar, shops, and huge observation wheel behind its property, Harrah's may find itself thrust into the hanging with the cool crowd, whether it wants it or not.

Carnaval Court, outside on the Strip's sidewalk, capitalizes on the street-party atmosphere with live bands and juggling bartenders. Just inside, Vegas icon Big Elvis often performs in the **Piano Bar,** which invites aspiring comedians and singers to the karaoke stage weekend evenings, and dueling keyboardists take over each night at 9pm.

Don't miss *Million Dollar Quartet* (Tues.-Wed. and Fri. 7pm, Mon. and Thurs. 5:30pm and 8pm, $72-100) which recreates the serendipitous star convergence-jam session with Elvis, Carl Perkins, Jerry Lee Lewis, and Johnny Cash. Even sixty years later (and with actors portraying the icons) the magic is still palpable. It's even kid-friendly!

The country superstar lends his name and unapologetic patriotism to **Toby Keith's I Love This Bar & Grill** (Sun.-Thurs. 11:30am-2am, Fri.-Sat. 11:30am-3am, $15-25). Try the fried bologna sandwich.

★ Caesars Palace

Restaurants: Bacchanal Buffet, Rao's, Nobu, Gordon Ramsay Pub & Grill, Central Michel Richard, Old Homestead Steakhouse, Payard Patisserie & Bistro, Serendipity 3, Mesa Grill, Empress Court, Cypress Street Marketplace, Beijing Noodle No. 9, Restaurant Guy Savoy
Entertainment: Shania Twain, Dr. Oz, Elton John's *Million Dollar Piano*, Absinthe, Matt Goss
Attractions: *Fall of Atlantis* and *Festival Fountain Show*, aquarium, Appian Way Shops, Forum Shops
Nightlife: Fizz Las Vegas, Shadow Bar, Cleopatra's Barge, Seahorse Lounge, Numb Bar & Frozen, Lobby Bar, Spanish Steps
Rome would probably look a lot like Las Vegas had it survived this long. **Caesars Palace** (3570 Las Vegas Blvd. S., 866/227-5938, $175-600 d) has incorporated all

the ancient empire's decadence and over-indulgence while adding a few thousand slot machines. Caesars opened with great fanfare in 1966 and has ruled the Strip ever since. Like the empire, it continues to expand, now boasting 3,348 guest rooms in six towers and 140,000 square feet of gaming space accented with marble, fountains, gilding, and royal reds. Wander the grounds searching for reproductions of some of the world's most famous statuary. The eagle-eyed might spy Michelangelo's *David* and Giambologna's *Rape of the Sabines* as well as the Brahma Shrine. The casino is so big that the website includes a "slot finder" application so gamblers can navigate to their favorite machines.

Cleopatra's Barge (Sun.-Thurs. 8pm-3am, Fri.-Sat. 11pm-3am), a floating lounge, attracts the full spectrum of the 21-and-over crowd for late-night bacchanalia. Carmine and gold accents only add to the decadence. Matt Goss (Fri.-Sat. 9:30pm, $50-120) takes the helm on weekend nights, making the women swoon with his original compositions and interpretations of the Great American Songbook.

All roads lead to the **Forum Shops** (Sun.-Thurs. 10am-11pm, Fri.-Sat. 10am-midnight), a collection of famous designer stores, specialty boutiques, and restaurants. Not all the shops are as froufrou as you might expect, but an hour here can do some serious damage to your bankroll. You'll also find the *Fall of Atlantis* and *Festival Fountain Show* (hourly Sun.-Thurs. 10am-11pm, Fri.-Sat. 10am-midnight, free), a multisensory, multimedia depiction of the gods' wrath.

If you (or your wallet) tire of Caesars's high-on-the-hog dining, nosh on British pub food at **Gordon Ramsay Pub and Grill** (Thurs.-Sun. 11am-11pm, Fri.-Sat. 11am-midnight). When in doubt, you can never go wrong with the fish-and-chips.

With so many guest rooms in six towers, it seems Caesars is always renovating somewhere. The sixth tower, Octavius,

opened in 2010, and the Palace Tower was overhauled in 2009. Most newer guest rooms are done in tan, wood, and marble. Ask for a south-facing room in the Augustus and Octavius tower to get commanding vistas of both the Bellagio fountains and the Strip.

Linq

Restaurants: Guy Fieri's Vegas Kitchen & Bar, Chayo Mexican Kitchen & Tequila Bar, Hash House a Go Go
Entertainment: Recycled Percussion, Divas Las Vegas, Jeff Civillico: Comedy in Action
Attractions: Auto Collection, O'Shea's
Nightlife: Catalyst Bar, Tag Sports Bar, Fat Tuesday

At **Linq** (3545 Las Vegas Blvd. S., 866/328-1888, $170-310 d), rooms are sleek and stylish. Pewter and chrome accented with eggplant, orange, or aqua murals evoke vintage Vegas. Other amenities include marble countertops, 47-inch flat-screen TVs, and iPod docks. But the hotel is really just a way to stay close to all the Gen X-focused boutiques, bars, and restaurants in the adjacent outdoor promenade.

The high point of this pedestrian-friendly plaza is **The High Roller,** the highest observation wheel in the world, but there's plenty more to warrant a stop. Two venues, **Brooklyn Bowl** and **F.A.M.E.** (Sun.-Thurs. noon-midnight, Fri.-Sat. noon-2am, $12-20) have you covered on all three eat, drink, and be merry points, combining dozens of beer taps with delectable noshes and live entertainment. F.A.M.E.'s Asian fusion—this ain't your college roommates' ramen—comes with generous helpings of Taiko drummers, dragon dancers, and other Asian-themed musical entertainment. Speaking of your college roommates, Vegas icon and locals' favorite **O'Shea's** (daily 24 hours) brings back the kegger party, with all its low-brow frivolity. Cheap drafts, beer pong tournaments, and Lucky the Leprechaun keep the festivities on the outdoor terrace raging well into the wee hours.

Recycled Percussion (Sat.-Thurs. 7pm, $60-80, children $36-47) makes drumming a participation sport. Guests receive a drumstick and an "instrument" and join in the junk rock jam session. The professionals on stage, "America's Got Talent" alumni, beat on anything they can find—ladders, paint buckets, even the kitchen sink, incorporating athleticism, dance, and humor.

Flamingo

Restaurants: Center Cut Steakhouse, Club Cappuccino, Hamada of Japan, Paradise Garden Buffet, Margaritaville, Carlos N Charlie's, Tropical Breeze Café, Beach Club Bar & Grill, Food Court
Entertainment: Donnie & Marie, Olivia Newton-John: *Summer Nights, Legends in Concert, X Burlesque,* Vinnie Favorito, XBU: X Burlesque University
Attractions: Wildlife Habitat
Nightlife: It's 5 O'clock Somewhere Bar, Garden Bar, Bugsy's Bar

Named for Virginia Hill, the long-legged girlfriend of Benjamin "don't call me Bugsy" Siegel, the **Flamingo** (3555 Las Vegas Blvd. S., 702/733-3111 or 800/732-2111, $150-290 d) has at turns embraced and shunned its gangster ties, which

the vertigo-inducing VooDoo Zipline at the Rio

stretch back to the 1960s. After Bugsy's (sorry, Mr. Siegel) Flamingo business practices ran afoul of the Cosa Nostra and led to his untimely end, Meyer Lansky took over. Mob ties continued to dog the property even after Kirk Kerkorian bought it to use as a training ground for his pride and joy, the International (now the Westgate). Hilton Hotels bought the Flamingo in 1970, giving the joint the legitimacy it needed. Today, its art deco architecture and pink-and-orange neon beckon pedestrians and conjure images of aging Mafiosi lounging by the pool, their tropical shirts half unbuttoned to reveal hairy chests and gold ropes. And that image seems just fine with the current owner, Caesars Entertainment, in a Vegas where the mob era is remembered almost fondly. Siegel's penthouse suite, behind the current hotel, has been replaced by the **Flamingo Wildlife Habitat** (daily 8am-dusk, free), where ibis, pelicans, turtles, koi fish, and, of course, Chilean flamingos luxuriate amid riparian plants and meandering streams.

Vinnie Favorito (daily 8pm, $61-66) channels Don Rickles in Bugsy's Cabaret, followed by the naughty nymphs of *X Burlesque* in the same venue (daily 10pm, $61-88). X performers reveal their seductive secrets at XBU—X Burlesque University (Sat. 3pm, $45). Would-be showgirls learn the art of the tease, from applying false eyelashes to pole dancing.

Guests can search for their lost shaker of salt in paradise at **Jimmy Buffett's Margaritaville** (Sun.-Thurs. 11am-2am, Fri.-Sat. 11am-3am, $20-30) while people-watching on the Strip and noshing on jambalaya and cheeseburgers.

The Flamingo recently completed the transformation of many of its guest rooms into "Go Rooms," dressed in swanky mahogany and white with bold swatches of hot pink. The rooms are smaller than those at other resorts but boast high-end entertainment systems. Suite options are just as colorful and include 42-inch TVs, wet bars, and all the other Vegas-sational accoutrements.

Rio

Restaurants: Royal India Bistro, Hash House a Go Go, Village Seafood Buffet, Martorano's, Voodoo Steakhouse, Búzio's Seafood Restaurant, KJ Dim Sum & Seafood, Wine Cellar & Tasting Room, All-American Bar & Grille, BK Whopper Bar, Pho Da Nang Vietnamese Kitchen, Sports Deli, Starbucks, Carnival World Buffet
Entertainment: Penn & Teller, Chippendales, The Eddie Griffin Experience, *MJ Live*, *The Rat Pack Is Back*, *X Rocks*
Attractions: VooDoo Zip Line, Masquerade Village
Nightlife: Masquerade Bar, IBar, Flirt Lounge, VooDoo Rooftop Nightclub & Lounge

A hit from the beginning, this carnival just off the Strip started expanding almost before its first 400-suite tower was complete in 1990. Now with three towers and 2,500 suites, the party's still raging with terrific buffets, beautiful-people magnet bars, and steamy shows. "Bevertainers" at the **Rio** (3700

W. Flamingo Rd., 866/746-7671, $99-260 d) take breaks from schlepping cocktails, taking turns on mini stages scattered throughout the casino to belt out tunes or gyrate to the music. Dancers and other performers may materialize at your slot machine to take your mind off your losses.

Beat it over to the Rio's Crown Theater for a **MJ Live** (daily 9pm, $53-78), a spot-on tribute to Michael Jackson. Michael Firestone nails the King of Pop's distinctive voice, mannerisms, and moonwalk. Kids are free with an adult purchase. **Flirt Lounge** (Sun.-Tues. and Thurs. 6:30pm-midnight, Fri.-Sat. 6:30pm-1am) and its easy-on-the-eyes waiters keep the Rio's Ultimate Girls Night Out churning. **VooDoo Lounge** (daily 9pm-late), 51 stories up, is just as hip.

Búzio's (Sun.-Thurs. 5pm-10pm, Fri.-Sat. 5pm-10:30pm, $25-45) has great crab-shack appetizers and buttery lobster and steak entrées.

All of the Rio's guest rooms are suites—a sofa and coffee table replace the uncomfortable easy chair found in most standard guest rooms. Rio suites measure about 650 square feet. The hotel's center-Strip location and room-tall windows make for exciting views.

Lower Strip
The Palms
Restaurants: N9NE Steakhouse, Lao Sze Chuan, Nove Italiano, Alizé, 24 Seven Café, Bistro Buffet, Fortunes, Simon
Entertainment: Brendan Theater
Nightlife: Ghostbar, Rojo Lounge, Social, Moon, The Mint, Tonic, Rain, Scarlet, The Lounge

The expression "party like a rock star" could have been invented for **The Palms** (4321 W. Flamingo Rd., 702/942-7777, $120-400 d). Penthouse views, uninhibited pool parties, lavish theme suites, and starring roles in MTV's *The Real World: Las Vegas* and Bravo's *Celebrity Poker Showdown* have brought notoriety and stars to the clubs, concert venue, and recording studio. **The Pearl** regularly hosts

the Bellagio's Conservatory

rock concerts. **Ghostbar** (daily 8pm-late), 55 floors atop the Ivory Tower, treats partiers vistas of the Strip and night sky. Frankly, my dear, **Scarlet**'s (Tues.-Sat. 6:30pm-late) Infusion Flight ($15) is a fun way to sample spice- and fruit-infused cocktails.

Andre Rochat's **Alizé** (daily 6pm, $45-70) is the quintessential French restaurant, authentic fare, snooty clientele, sophisticated decor, and top-of-the-world views.

The Fantasy Tower houses the fantasy suites, while the original tower offers large guest rooms. They are nothing special to look at, but the feathery beds and luxurious comforters make it easy to roll over and go back to sleep, even if you're not nursing a hangover. The newest tower, Palms Place, is part of the Las Vegas "condotel" trend. Its 599 studios and one-bedrooms, restaurant, spa, and pool offer opportunities to recuperate from the partying.

Bellagio

Restaurants: Jasmine, Le Cirque, Michael Mina, Picasso, Prime Steakhouse, Circo, Sensi, Yellowtail, Todd English's Olives, Fix, Noodles, The Buffet, Café Bellagio, Pool Café, Café Gelato, Palio, Snacks, Jean Philippe Patisserie
Entertainment: Cirque du Soleil's *O*
Attractions: The Fountains at Bellagio, The Conservatory, Bellagio Gallery of Fine Art, Fiori di Como
Nightlife: The Bank, Hyde, Lily Bar & Lounge, Petrossian Bar, Baccarat Bar, Pool Bar, Starting Gate

With nearly 4,000 guest rooms and suites, ★ **Bellagio** (3600 Las Vegas Blvd. S., 702/693-7444 or 888/987-6667, $220-450 d) boasts a population larger than the village perched on Lake Como from which it borrows its name. And to keep pace with its Italian namesake, Bellagio created an 8.5-acre lake between the hotel and Las Vegas Boulevard. The view of the lake and its **Fountains at Bellagio** (Mon.-Fri. 3pm-midnight, Sat.-Sun. noon-midnight) are free, as is the aromatic fantasy that is **Bellagio**

Conservatory (daily 24 hours). And the **Bellagio Gallery of Fine Art** (daily 10am-7pm, $11-16) would be a bargain at twice the price—you can spend an edifying day at one of the world's priciest resorts (including a cocktail and lunch) for less than $50. Even if you don't spring for gallery admission, art demands your attention throughout the hotel and casino. The glass flower petals in Dale Chihuly's *Fiori di Como* sculpture bloom from the lobby ceiling, foreshadowing the opulent experiences to come.

The display of artistry continues but the bargains end at **Via Bellagio** (daily 10am-midnight), the resort's shopping district, including heavyweight retailers Armani, Prada, Chanel, Tiffany, and their ilk.

Would you like not only to eat like a gourmand, but to cook like one too? **An Executive Chef's Culinary Classroom** ($125) is your own private Food Network special. The resort's chefs provide step-by-step instructions as guests prepare appetizers, entrées, and desserts at their own work stations.

Befitting Bellagio's world-class status, intriguing and expensive restaurants abound. **Michael Mina** (Sun.-Tues. and Thurs. 5:30pm-10pm, Fri.-Sat. 5pm-10:15pm, $45-60) is worth the price. Restrained decor adds to the simple elegance of the cuisine, which is mostly American beef and seafood with European and Asian influences. Traditional Asian dishes are the specialty at **Noodles** (daily 11am-2am, $15-20), if you're in search of something more affordable.

Bellagio's tower rooms are the epitome of luxury, with Italian marble, oversize bathtubs, remote-controlled drapes, Egyptian-cotton sheets, and 510 square feet in which to spread out. The sage-plum and indigo-silver color schemes are refreshing changes from the goes-with-everything beige and the camouflages-all-stains paisley often found on the Strip.

Paris

Restaurants: Burger Brasserie, Sugar Factory Bar & Grill, Mon Ami Gabi, Martorano's, Gordon Ramsay Steak, Eiffel Tower Restaurant, Café Belle Madeleine, La Creperie, JJ's Boulangerie, Le Café Ile St. Louis, Le Village Buffet, Yong Kang Street

Entertainment: *Jersey Boys*, Anthony Cools

Attractions: Eiffel Tower

Nightlife: Napoleon's Lounge, Le Cabaret, Le Central, Le Bar du Sport, Gustav's, Chateau Nightclub & Rooftop

Designers used Gustav Eiffel's original drawings to ensure that the half-size version that anchors **Paris Las Vegas** (3655 Las Vegas Blvd. S., 877/242-6753, $150-300 d) conformed—down to the last cosmetic rivet—to the original. That attention to detail prevails throughout this property, which works hard to evoke the City of Light, from large-scale reproductions of the Arc de Triomphe, Champs Élysées, and Louvre to more than half a dozen French restaurants. The tower is perhaps the most romantic spot in town to view the Strip; you'll catch your breath as the elevator whisks you to the observation deck 460 feet up, then have it taken away again by the lights from one of the most famous skylines in the world. Back at street level, the cobblestone lanes and brass streetlights of **Le Boulevard** (daily 10am-11pm) invite shoppers into quaint shops and "sidewalk" patisseries. The casino offers its own attractions, not the least of which is the view of the Eiffel Tower's base jutting through the ceiling.

The **Paris Theatre** hosts headliners. **Anthony Cools—The Uncensored Hypnotist** (Tues. and Thurs.-Sun. 9pm, $40-65) cajoles his mesmerized subjects through very adult simulations.

You'll be wishing you had packed your beret when you order a beignet and cappuccino at **Le Café Ile St. Louis** (daily 6pm-11pm, $20-35). While the look and feel are French sidewalk café, the menu tends toward American.

Standard guest rooms in the 33-story tower are decorated in a rich earth-tone palette and have marble baths. There's nothing Left Bank bohemian about them, however. The guest rooms exude little flair and little personality, but the simple, quality furnishings make Paris a moderately priced option in the middle of a top-dollar neighborhood.

Cosmopolitan

Restaurants: Blue Ribbon Sushi Bar & Grill, China Poblano, Comme Ca, D.O.C.G., Estiatorio Milos, Holsteins, Jaleo, Overlook Grill, Scarpetta, Secret Pizza, STK, The Henry, Va Bene Caffè, Wicked Spoon

Attractions: Public art

Nightlife: Rose. Rabbit. Lie, The Chandelier, Vesper, Book & Stage, Bond, Queue Bark, The Neapolitan, Marquee Nightclub & Day Club

Marble bath floors and big soaking tubs in 460-square-foot rooms evoke urban penthouse living at ★ **Cosmopolitan** (3708 Las Vegas Blvd. S., 702/698-7000, $280-440 d). Because it's too cool to host production shows, the resort's entertainment schedule mixes DJs of the moment with the most laid-back headliners (Bruno Mars and John Legend have graced the stage).

That nouveau riche attitude carries through to the restaurant and nightlife offerings. **Rose. Rabbit. Lie.** (Tues.-Sat. 5:30pm-2am, $80-150) is equal parts supper club, nightclub, and jazz club. Throughout the evening bluesy, jazzy torch singers, magicians, tap and hip-hop dancers, and a talented, if a touch loud, klezmer band keep the joint jumping. **Vesper Bar** (daily 24 hours), named for James Bond's favorite martini, prides itself on serving hipster versions of classic (and sometimes forgotten) cocktails. Possibly the best day club in town, **Marquee** (11am-6pm) on the roof, brings in the beautiful people with DJs and sweet bungalow lofts. When darkness falls, the day club becomes an extension of the pulsating Marquee nightclub.

Aria

Restaurants: Aria Café, BarMasa, Blossom, the Buffet, Five50, Javier's, Jean Georges Steakhouse, Jean Philippe Patisserie, Julian Serrano, Lemongrass, The

Roasted Bean, Sage, Sirio, Starbucks, Tetsu
Entertainment: Cirque du Soleil's *Zarkana*
Attractions: Public art, Crystals
Nightlife: Haze, Gold Lounge, Deuce Lounge, Alibi, Baccarat Lounge, High Limit Lounge, Lift Bar, Lobby Bar, Pool Bar

All glass and steel, ultra-modern ★ **Aria** (3730 Las Vegas Blvd. S., 702/590-7757, $210-500) would look more at home in Manhattan than Las Vegas. Touchpads control the drapes, the lighting, and the climate in Aria's chocolate- or grape-paletted guest rooms—one touch transforms the room into sleep mode. A traditional hotel casino, Aria shares the City Center umbrella with **Vdara,** a Euro-chic boutique hotel with no gaming.

Guests are invited to browse an extensive public art collection, with works by Maya Lin, Jenny Holzer, and Richard Long, among others. **Crystals,** a 500,000-square-foot mall lets you splurge among hanging gardens. Restaurants fronted by Bobby Flay, Wolfgang Puck, and Todd English take the place of Sbarro's and Cinnabon.

Culinary genius Masa Takayama guarantees that **BarMasa**'s (Thurs.-Tues. 5pm-11pm, $18-40) bluefin goes from the Sea of Japan to your spicy tuna roll in less than 24 hours.

Hard Rock

Restaurants: 35 Steaks+Martinis, Culinary Dropout, Fu Asian Kitchen, Mr. Lucky's, Nobu, Pink Taco, Juice Bar, Fuel Café
Entertainment: The Joint, Soundwaves, Vinyl
Nightlife: Rehab Pool Party, Body English, The Ainsworth, Vanity, Center Bar, Luxe Bar, Midway Bar

Young stars and the media-savvy 20-somethings who idolize them contribute to the frat party mojo at the **Hard Rock** (4455 Paradise Rd., 800/473-7625, $170-320 d) and the spring-break atmosphere poolside. While the casino is shaped like a record, if your music collection dates back to records, this probably isn't the place for you. The gaming tables and machines are located in the "record

deluxe room at Aria

abel" and the shops and restaurants are n the "grooves."

Contemporary and classic rockers egularly grace the stage at the **Joint** and arty with their fans at **Body English** Thurs.-Sun. 10:30pm-4am). **Vanity** Thurs.-Sun. 10pm-4am) is a little more efined, with a 20,000-crystal chandeier that showers sparkles on the sunken lance floor.

The provocatively named **Pink Taco** Mon.-Thurs. 11am-10pm, Fri.-Sat. 11amnidnight, Sun. 9am-10pm, $15-25) dishes ip Mexican and Caribbean specialties.

Several rounds of expansion have rought the resort's room count to a Vegas-respectable 1,500. Guest rooms are lecorated in mint and include stocked ninibars, Bose CD sound systems and blasma TVs, as befitting wannabe rock tars.

New York New York

Restaurants: Nine Fine Irishmen, Gallagher's teakhouse, Il Fornaio, Chin Chin Café & Sushi,

Gonzalez y Gonzalez, America, 48th and Crepe, Nathan's Hot Dogs, New York Pizzeria, Broadway Burger Bar, Quick Bites, MGM Grand Buffet
Entertainment: Cirque du Soleil's *Zumanity*, Blue Man Group
Attractions: Hershey's Chocolate World, Big Apple Coaster & Arcade, CSI: The Experience
Nightlife: Bar at Times Square, Center Bar, Coyote Ugly, Pour 24, Big Chill, High Limit Bar, Lobby Bar

One look at this loving tribute to the city that never sleeps and you won't be able to fuhgedaboutit. From the city skyline outside (the skyscrapers contain the resort's hotel rooms) to laundry hanging between crowded faux brownstones indoors, **New York New York** (3790 Las Vegas Blvd. S., 866/815-4365, $130-250 d) will have even grizzled Gothamites feeling like they've come home again. Window air conditioners in the Greenwich Village apartments evoke the city's gritty heat.

The **Big Apple Coaster** (Sun.-Thurs. 11am-11pm, Fri.-Sat. 10:30am-midnight, $14) winds its way around the resort, an experience almost as hair-raising as a New York City cab ride, which the coaster cars are painted to resemble. **Big Apple Arcade** (daily 8am-midnight) has games of skill and luck, motion simulators, and rides.

Dueling pianists keep **The Bar at Times Square** (daily 11am-2:30am) rocking into the wee hours, and the sexy bar staff at **Coyote Ugly** (Sun.-Thurs. 6pm-2am, Fri.-Sat. 6pm-3am) defies its name.

New York New York's 2,023 guest rooms are standard size, 350-500 square feet. The roller coaster zooms around the towers, so you might want to ask for a room out of earshot.

MGM Grand

Restaurants: Joël Robuchon, L'Atelier de Joël Robuchon, Hakkasan, Tom Colicchio's Craftsteak, Emeril's Fiamma, Pearl, Shibuya, Wolfgang Puck Bar & Grill, Crush, Hecho en Vegas, Grand Wok and Sushi Bar, MGM Grand Buffet, Rainforest Café, Michael Mina Pub 1842, Avenue Café, Tap Sports Bar, Cabana Grill, Stage Deli, Starbucks, Corner Cakes, Blizz, Project Pie, Food Court

Entertainment: Cirque du Soleil's *Kà*, David Copperfield, Brad Garrett's Comedy Club, Beacher's Madhouse

Attractions: CSI: The Experience, the Roller Coaster at New York New York, CBS Television City Research Center

Nightlife: Centrifuge, Rouge, Lobby Bar, Wet Republic Ultra Pool, Whiskey Down, West Wing Bar

Gamblers enter **MGM Grand** (3799 Las Vegas Blvd. S., 888/646-1203, $160-350 d) through portals guarded by MGM's mascot, the 45-foot-tall king of the jungle. The uninitiated may feel like a gazelle on the savanna, swallowed by the 171,000-square-foot casino floor, the largest in Las Vegas. But the watering hole, MGM's 6.5-acre pool complex, is relatively predator-free. MGM capitalizes on the movie studio's greatest hits. Even the hotel's emerald facade evokes the magical city in *The Wizard of Oz*.

Most of the pop star impressionists, strippers, and acrobats are little people at **Beacher's Madhouse** (Thurs.-Sat. 10:30pm, $75-125). One gets shot out of a cannon, others gyrate and cavort as Miley Cyrus and Lady Gaga. Part vaudeville, part circus sideshow, the Madhouse on a given night may include magic, Sesame Street characters, and a woman who crushes beer cans with her breasts. Just another night in Vegas.

Boob tube fans can volunteer for studies at the **CBS Television City Research Center** (daily 10am-8:30pm, free), where they can screen pilots for shows under consideration by the network. And if your favorite show happens to revolve around solving crimes, don some rubber gloves and search for clues at **CSI: The Experience** (daily 9am-9pm, age 12 and up $28, age 4-11 $21, not recommended for children under age 12). Three crime scenes keep the experience fresh.

MGM Grand houses enough top restaurants for a week of gourmet dinners. If you only have time (or budget) to try one, make it **Shibuya** (Sun.-Thurs. 5:30pm-10pm, Fri.-Sat. 5:30pm-10:30pm,

crime scene at MGM Grand's CSI: The Experience

$70-100). The sushi and sashimi will draw the eye, but you do yourself a disservice if you don't order the pork belly.

Standard guest rooms in the Grand Tower are filled with the quality furnishings you'd expect in Las Vegas's upscale hotels. The West Tower guest rooms are smaller, at 350 square feet, but exude the swinging style of an upscale Hollywood studio apartment crammed with a CD and DVD player and other high-tech gizmos; those in the Grand Tower are more traditional.

Tropicana

Restaurants: Bacio Italian Cuisine, Biscayne, Beach Café, South Beach Food Court
Entertainment: Laugh Factory, Murray: Celebrity Magician, *Tropicana Nights*
Attractions: Xposed!
Nightlife: Tropicana Lounge, Lucky's Sports Bar, Coconut Grove Bar

When it opened at in 1959, the **Tropicana** (801 Las Vegas Blvd. S., 888/381-8767, $110-210 d) was the most luxurious, most

expensive resort on the Strip. It has survived several boom-and-bust cycles since then, and its decor reflects the willy-nilly expansion and refurbishment efforts through the years. Today, the rooms have bright, airy South Beach themes with plantation shutters and light wood, 42-inch plasma TVs, and iPod docks.

The beach chic atmosphere include a two-acre pool complex with reclining deck chairs and swim-up blackjack. On summer Saturdays (noon-7pm) the deck hosts **Xposed!,** a gay pool party with sand volleyball, go-go dancers, and trendy DJs.

America's Got Talent alum **Murray: Celebrity Magician** (Sun.-Thurs. 4pm and 7pm, $35-45) wows audiences with up-close sleight of hand and big production tricks, bantering amiably all the while. Showtimes, prices, and the performance are kid-friendly.

Luxor

Restaurants: Tender Steak & Seafood, Rice & Company, Public House, T&T Tacos & Tequila, More Buffet, Pyramid Café, Backstage Deli, Food Court, Blizz, Burger Bar, Ri Ra Irish Pub, Slice of Vegas, Hussong's Cantina
Entertainment: Jabbawockeez, Criss Angel: *Believe*, Carrot Top, *Fantasy, Menopause The Musical*
Attractions: Bodies . . . the Exhibition, *Titanic:* The Artifact Exhibition
Nightlife: LAX, Savile Row, Centra, Aurora, Flight, High Bar, PlayBar

Other than its pyramid shape and name, not much remains of the Egyptian theme at the **Luxor** (3900 Las Vegas Blvd. S., 877/386-4658, $50-175 d). Much of the mummy-and-scarab decor was swept away. In its place are upscale and decidedly post-pharaoh nightclubs, restaurants, and shops. Many are located on the sky bridge between Luxor and Mandalay Bay. What remains are the large, 120,000-square-foot casino and 4,400 guest rooms in the pyramid and twin 22-story towers. You can also see the largest atrium in the world, an intense light beam that is visible from space, and inclinators—elevators that move along the building's oblique angles.

Magic meets magic mushrooms in the surrealistic, psychedelic dream sequences of Criss Angel in *Believe* (702/262-4400 or 800/557-7428, Wed.-Thurs. 7pm, Tues. and Fri.-Sat. 7pm and 9:30pm, $65-143). The Atrium Showroom (702/262-4400 or 800/557-7428) is home to *Fantasy* (daily 10:30pm, $42-65), a typical jiggle-and-tease topless review with some singing and comedy thrown in; *Menopause the Musical* (Tues. 5pm and 8:30pm, Wed.-Mon. 5:30pm, $55-70), a musical salute to the change; and the comedian and prop jockey **Carrot Top** (Mon. and Wed.-Sun. 8pm, $55-66).

Old-school touches such as chandeliers and red leather sofas contrast the young and flat-bellied guests at **LAX** (Wed. and Fri.-Sat. 5pm-late).

The hotel's pyramid shape makes for interesting room features, such as a slanted exterior wall, as well as a few challenges. Tower rooms are more traditional in their shape, decor, and amenities.

Mandalay Bay

Restaurants: Aureole, Border Grill, Burger Bar, Charlie Palmer Steak, Citizens Kitchen & Bar, Crossroads at House of Blues, Fleur, Kumi, Lupo, Mix, Press, RM Seafood, Stripsteak, Bayside Buffet, Beach Bar & Grill, Yogurt In, Starbucks, House of Blues Foundation Room, Hussong's Cantina, Mizuya, Noodle Shop, Raffles Café, Red Square, Boiler Room
Entertainment: *Michael Jackson ONE*
Attractions: Shark Reef
Nightlife: Light, Daylight Beach Club, Bikini Bar, Evening Call, Eyecandy Sound Lounge, Fat Tuesday, Minus 5 Ice Lounge, Mix Lounge, Orchid Lounge, Press, Ri Ra Irish Pub, The Lounge, Verandah Lounge, 1923 Bourbon & Burlesque

Enter this South Pacific behemoth at the southern tip of the Las Vegas Strip and try to comprehend its mind-boggling statistics. ★ **Mandalay Bay** (3950 Las Vegas Blvd. S., 877/632-7800, $145-300 d) has one of the largest casino floors in

Mandalay Bay's Daylight Beach Club

the world at 135,000 square feet. Wander into Mandalay's beach environment, an 11-acre paradise comprising three pools, a lazy river, and a 1.6-million-gallon wave pool complete with a real beach made of five million pounds of sand. There's also a tops-optional sunbathing pool deck. You could spend your entire vacation in the pool area, gambling at the beach's three-level casino, eating at its restaurant, shopping for pool gear at the poolside stand, and loading up on sandals and bikinis at the nearby Pearl Moon boutique. The beach hosts a concert series during summer.

When you're ready to check out the rest of the property, don't miss **House of Blues** (hours vary by event), with live blues, rock, and acoustic sets as well as DJs spinning dance tunes.

Mandalay Place (daily 10am-11pm), on the sky bridge between Mandalay Bay and Luxor, is smaller and less hectic than other casino malls. Unusual shops such as The Guinness Store, where fans can pick up merchandise celebrating their favorite Irish stout, share space with eateries and high-concept bars like **Minus 5** (daily 11am-3am), where barflies don parkas before entering the below-freezing (23°F) establishment. The glasses aren't just frosted; they're fashioned completely out of ice.

An urban hip-hop worldview and the King of Pop's unmatched talent guide the vignettes in *Michael Jackson ONE* (Fri.-Tues. 7pm and 9:30pm, Sun. 4:30pm and 7pm, $69-160). Michael's musical innovation and the Cirque du Soleil trademark aerial and acrobatic acts pay homage to the human spirit.

Sheathed in Indian artifacts and crafts, the **Foundation Room** (daily 11pm-late) is just as dark and mysterious as the subcontinent, with private rooms, a dining room, and several bars catering to various musical tastes.

Vegas pays tribute to Paris, Rome, New York, and Venice, so why not Moscow? Round up your comrades for caviar and vodka as well as continental favorites at **Red Square** (Sun.-Thurs. 5pm-10pm, Fri.-Sat. 5pm-11pm, $25-40). Look for the headless Lenin statue at the entrance.

Standard guest rooms are chic and roomy (550 square feet), with warm fabrics and plush bedding. The guest rooms are nothing special visually, but the baths are fit for royalty, with huge tubs, glass-walled showers, and king's-and-queen's commodes. To go upscale, check out the Delano boutique hotel; for very upscale, book at the Four Seasons—both are part of the same complex.

Downtown
Binion's

Restaurants: Top of Binions Steakhouse, Binion's Deli, Binion's Café, Benny's Smokin BBZ & Brews

Before Vegas became a destination resort city, it catered to inveterate gamblers, hard drinkers, and others on the fringes of society. Ah, the good old days! A gambler himself, Benny Binion put his place in the middle of downtown, a magnet for the serious player, offering high limits and few frills. **Binion's** (128 Fremont St., 702/382-1600) still offers single-deck blackjack and a poker room frequented by grizzled veterans. While Binion's and the rest of Las Vegas have been overtaken by Strip megaresorts, the little den on Fremont Street still retains the flavor of Old Vegas, though the Binion family is no longer involved. Harrah's bought the place in 2004.

The hotel at Binion's closed in 2009, but the casino and restaurants remain open, including the **Top of Binion's Steakhouse** (daily 5pm-10pm, $30-55), famous for its Fremont Street views and aged black Angus.

Golden Nugget

Restaurants: Vic & Anthony's, Chart House, Grotto, Lillie's Asian Cuisine, Red Sushi, Cadillac Mexican Kitchen & Tequila Bar, Buffet, The Grille, Claim Jumper, Starbucks

Entertainment: Gordie Brown

Attractions: Hand of Faith, Shark Tank

Nightlife: Rush Lounge, Gold Diggers, H2O Bar at the Tank, Claude's Bar, Ice Bar, Bar 46

Considered by many to be the only Strip-worthy resort downtown, the ★ **Golden Nugget** (129 E. Fremont St., 800/634-3454, $89-179) has been a fixture for nearly 70 years, beckoning diners and gamblers with gold leaf and a massive gold nugget. Landry's, the restaurant chain and new Nugget owner, has embarked on an ambitious campaign to maintain the hotel's opulence, investing $300 million for casino expansion, more restaurants and a new 500-room hotel tower.

If you don't feel like swimming with the sharks in the poker room, you can get up close and personal with their finned namesakes at the **Golden Nugget Pool** (daily 10am-5pm, free), an outdoor pool with a three-story waterslide that takes riders through the hotel's huge aquarium, home to sharks, rays, and other exotic marine life. Bathers can also swim up to the aquarium for a face-to-face with the aquatic predators, or schedule a guided tour ($30). Waterfalls and lush landscaping help make this one of the world's best hotel pools.

Gold Diggers nightclub (Wed.-Sun. 9pm-late) plays hip-hop, pop, and classic rock for the dancing pleasure of guests and go-go girls.

When checking in, pause to have your picture taken with the **Hand of Faith,** a 62-pound gold nugget. Rooms are appointed in dark wood and chocolate hues.

Sights

Downtown
★ Fremont Street Experience

With land at a premium and more and more tourists flocking to the opulence of the Strip, downtown Las Vegas in the last quarter of the 20th century found its lights beginning to flicker. Enter **Fremont Street Experience** (702/678-5777), an ambitious plan to transform downtown and its tacky "Glitter Gulch" reputation into a pedestrian-friendly enclave. Highlighted by a four-block-long canopy festooned with 12 million light-emitting diodes 90 feet in the air, Fremont Street Experience is downtown's answer to the Strip's erupting volcanoes and fantastic dancing fountains. The canopy, dubbed Viva Vision, runs atop Fremont Street between North Main Street and North 4th Street.

Once an hour, the promenade goes dark and all heads lift toward the canopy, supported by massive concrete pillars. For six minutes, visitors are enthralled by the multimedia shows that chronicle Western history, span the careers of classic rock bands, or transport viewers to fantasy worlds. Viva Vision runs several different shows daily, on the hour from dusk to 1am.

Before and after the light shows, strolling buskers sing for their supper, artists create five-minute masterpieces, and caricaturists airbrush souvenir

DOWNTOWN LAS VEGAS

ORAN K GRAGSON HWY

MESQUITE AVE

MAIN STREET STATION

MOB MUSEUM

E STEWART AVE

CALIFORNIA

E OGDEN AVE

FREMONT

BINION'S

FREMONT STREET EXPERIENCE

EL CORTEZ

PLAZA

E FREMONT ST.

GOLDEN GATE

GOLDEN NUGGET

FOUR QUEENS

FITZGERALDS

E CARSON AVE

0   200 yds
0   200 m

E BRIDGER AVE

AVALON TRAVEL

↓ To Arts Factory

portraits. Fremont Street hosts top musical acts, including some A-listers during big Las Vegas weekends such as National Finals Rodeo, NASCAR races, and New Year. The adjacent Fremont East Entertainment District houses quirky eateries, clubs, and art galleries.

Las Vegas Natural History Museum

Las Vegas boasts a volcano, a pyramid, and even a Roman coliseum, so it's little wonder that an animatronic *Tyrannosaurus rex* calls the valley home too. Dedicated to "global life forms . . . from the desert to the ocean, from Nevada to Africa, from prehistoric times to the present," the **Las Vegas Natural History Museum** (900 Las Vegas Blvd. N., 702/384-3466, daily 9am-4pm, adults $10, seniors, military, and students $8, ages 3-11 $5) is filled with rotating exhibits that belie the notion that Las Vegas culture begins and ends with neon casino signs.

Visitors to the Treasures of Egypt gallery can enter a realistic depiction of King Tut's tomb to study archeological techniques and discover golden treasures of the pharaohs. The Wild Nevada gallery showcases the raw beauty and surprisingly varied life forms of the Mojave Desert. Interactive exhibits also enlighten visitors on subjects such as marine life, geology, African ecosystems, and more.

The 35-foot-long *T. rex* and his friends (rivals? entrées?)—a triceratops, a raptor, and an ichthyosaur—greet visitors in the Prehistoric Life gallery. And by "greet" we mean a bloodcurdling roar from the *T. rex*, so take precautions with the little ones and the faint of heart.

Neon Museum and Boneyard

Book a one-hour guided tour of the Neon Museum and Boneyard (770 Las Vegas Blvd. N., 702/387-6366, daily 10am-3pm and 5pm-7pm, $18-25) and take a trip to Las Vegas's more recent past. The boneyard displays 200 old neon signs that were used to advertise casinos, restaurants, bars, and even a flower shop. Several have been restored to their former glory. The visitors center (daily 9:30am-8pm) is housed in the relocated scallop-shaped lobby of the historic La Concha Motel. You can skip the boneyard and take a free self-guided tour of nine restored signs displayed as public art. Note that the neighborhood can be sketchy.

Neon Park, just behind the clamshell visitors center, includes interpretive signage, benches, picnic tables, and a "NEON" sign created from the N's from the Golden Nugget and Desert Inn, the E from Caesars Palace, and the O from Binion's.

Lied Discovery Children's Museum

Voted Best Museum in Las Vegas by readers of the local newspaper, the three-story Lied Discovery Children's Museum (360 Promenade Pl., 702/382-5437, Tues.-Fri. 9am-4pm, Sat. 10am-5pm, Sun. noon-5pm, $12) presents more than 100 interactive scientific, artistic, and life-skill activities. Children enjoy themselves so much that they forget they're learning. Among the best permanent exhibits is *It's Your Choice*, which shows kids the importance of eating right and adopting a healthy lifestyle. Exhibits show kids creative ways to explore their world: drama, cooperation, dance, and visual arts. *The Summit* is the playground jungle gym on steroids—13 levels of slides, ladders, tubes, and interactive experiments.

Mormon Fort

The tiny Mormon Fort (500 E. Washington Ave., 702/486-3511, Tues.-Sat. 8am-4:30pm, $1, under 12 free) is the oldest building in Las Vegas. The adobe remnant, constructed by Mormon missionaries in 1855, was part of their original settlement, which they abandoned in 1858. It then served as a store, a barracks, and a shed on the Gass-Stewart Ranch. After that, the railroad leased the old fort to various tenants, including the Bureau of Reclamation, which stabilized and rebuilt the shed to use as a concrete-testing laboratory for Hoover Dam. In 1955 the railroad sold the old fort to the Elks, who in 1963 bulldozed the whole wooden structure (except the little remnant) into the ranch swimming pool and torched it. The shed was bought by the city in 1971.

Since then, a number of preservation societies have helped keep it in place. The museum includes a visitors center, a recreation of the original fort built around the remnant. A tour guide presents the history orally while display boards provide it visually. Your visit will not go unrewarded—it's immensely refreshing to see some preservation of the past in this city of the ultimate now.

★ Mob Museum

The Museum of Organized Crime and Law Enforcement (300 Stewart Ave., 702/229-2734, http://themobmuseum.org, Sun.-Thurs. 10am-7pm, Fri.-Sat. 10am-8pm, adults $20, over age 64 $16, age 11-17 $14, under age 11 free) celebrates Las Vegas's Mafia past and the cops and agents who finally ran the mob out of town. The museum is located inside the city's downtown post office and courthouse, appropriately the site of the 1951 Kefauver Hearing investigating organized crime.

Displays include the barber chair where Albert Anastasia was gunned down while getting a haircut, and an examination of the violence, ceremony, and hidden meanings behind Mafia "hits," all against a grisly background—the wall from Chicago's St. Valentine's Day Massacre that spelled the end of six members of Bugs Moran's crew and one hanger-on. *Bringing Down the Mob* displays the tools federal agents used—wiretaps, surveillance, and weapons—to clean up the town.

Downtown Arts District

Centered at South Main Street and East Charleston Boulevard, the district gives art lovers a concentration of galleries to suit any taste, plus an eclectic mix of shops, eateries, and other surprises. The Arts Factory (107 E. Charleston Blvd., 702/383-3133), a two-story redbrick industrial building, is the district's birthplace. It hosts exhibitions, drawing classes, and poetry readings. Tenants include a toy shop, a yoga studio, a comic books store, a roller-skate store, and galleries and studios belonging to artists working in every media and genre imaginable. One downstairs space, Jana's RedRoom (Sun. and Wed.-Thurs. 11am-4pm, Fri.-Sat. 4pm-8pm) displays and sells canvasses by local artists.

Virtually all the galleries and other paeans to urban pop culture participate in Las Vegas's First Friday (every month 1st Fri. 5pm-11pm) event, but otherwise galleries keep limited hours, so if there's something you don't want to miss, call for an appointment.

At the southern edge of the District, browse the edgy, often avant-garde displays at Blackbird Studios (1551 S. Commerce St., 702/678-6278) and neighboring Circadian Gallery, with its aggressive, brooding expressions and impressionistic nudes by Daniel Pearson.

Center Strip
Madame Tussauds

Ever wanted to dunk over Shaq? Marry George Clooney? Leave Simon Cowell speechless? Madame Tussauds (3377 Las Vegas Blvd. S., 702/862-7800, www.madametussauds.com/lasvegas, daily 10am-10pm, adults $30, age 4-12 $20, under age 4 free) at The Venetian Hotel gives you your chance. Unlike most other museums, Madame Tussauds encourages guests to get up close and "personal" with the world leaders, sports heroes, and screen stars immortalized in wax. Photo ops and interactive activities abound. With *Karaoke Revolution Presents: American Idol* you can take to the stage and then hear Simon Cowell and Ryan Seacrest's thoughts on your burgeoning singing career. The crowd roars as you take it to the rack and sink the game-winner over Shaquille O'Neal's vainly outstretch arm. You'll feel right at home in the "mansion" as you don bunny ears and lounge on the circular bed with Hugh Hefner.

★ Gondola Rides

We dare you not to sigh at the grandeur of Venice in the desert as you pass beneath quaint bridges and idyllic sidewalk cafés, your gondolier serenading you with the accompaniment of the Grand Canal's gurgling wavelets. The indoor gondolas (3355 Las Vegas Blvd. S., 702/607-3982, Sun.-Thurs. 10am-11pm, Fri.-Sat. 10am-midnight, $19 for 0.5 miles) skirt the Grand Canal Shoppes inside The Venetian Hotel under the mall's painted-sky ceiling fresco. Outdoor gondolas (daily noon-11pm, weather permitting, $19) skim The Venetian's 31,000-square-foot lagoon for 12 minutes, giving riders a unique perspective on the Las Vegas Strip. Plying the waters at regular intervals, the realistic-looking gondolas seat four, but couples who don't want to share a boat can pay double.

★ Secret Garden and Dolphin Habitat

It's no mirage—those really are pure-white tigers lounging in their own plush resort on the Mirage casino floor.

Legendary Las Vegas magicians Siegfried and Roy, who have dedicated much of their lives to preserving big cats, opened the **Secret Garden** (Mirage, 3400 Las Vegas Blvd. S., 702/791-7188, daily 11am-5pm, adults $20, age 4-12 $15, under age 4 free) in 1990. In addition to the milky-furred tigers, the garden is home to blue-eyed, black-striped white tigers as well as panthers, lions, and leopards. Although caretakers don't "perform" with the animals, if your visit is well-timed, you could see the cats playing, wrestling, and even swimming in their pristine waterfall-fed pools. The cubs in the specially built nursery are sure to register high on the cuteness meter.

Visit the Atlantic bottlenoses at the **Dolphin Habitat** right next door, also in the middle of the Mirage's palm trees and jungle foliage. The aquatic mammals don't perform on cue either, but they're natural hams, and often interact with their visitors, nodding their heads in response to trainer questions, turning aerial somersaults, and "walking" on their tails across the water. An underwater viewing area provides an unusual perspective into the dolphins' world. Feeding times are a hoot.

Budding naturalists (age 13 and over who are willing to part with $595) won't want to miss Dolphin Habitat's Trainer for a Day program, which allows them to feed, swim with, and pose for photos with some of the aquatic stars while putting them through their daily regimen.

★ High Roller

Taller than even the London Eye, the 550-foot **High Roller** (Linq, 3535 Las Vegas Blvd. S., 702/777-2782 or 866/574-3851, daily noon-2am, $20-35) is the highest observation wheel in the world. Two thousand LED lights dance in intricate choreography among the ride's spokes and pods. The dazzling view from 50 stories up is unparalleled. Ride at night for a perfect panorama of the famous Strip skyline. Ride at dusk for inspiring glimpses of the desert sun setting over the mountains. Forty passengers fit in each of the High Roller's 28 compartments, lessening wait time for the half-hour ride circuit. During "happy half hour" (4pm-7pm $25; 10pm-1am $40) passengers can board special bar cars and enjoy unlimited cocktails during the ride.

Lower Strip
Showcase Mall

"Mall" is an overly ambitious moniker for the **Showcase Mall** (3785 Las Vegas Blvd. S.), a mini diversion on the Strip. The centerpiece, the original **M&M's World** (702/736-7611, daily 9am-midnight, free), underwent a 2010 expansion and now includes a printing station where customers can customize their bite-size treats with words and pictures. The 3,300-square-foot expansion on the third floor of the store, which originally opened in 1997, includes additional opportunities to stock up on all things M: Swarovski crystal candy dishes, an M&M guitar, T-shirts, and purses made from authentic M&M wrappers. The addition brings the chocoholic's paradise to more than 30,000 square feet, offering key chains, coffee mugs, lunch boxes, and the addicting treats in every color imaginable. Start with a viewing of the short 3-D film, *I Lost My M in Las Vegas.* A replica of Kyle Busch's M&M-sponsored No. 18 NASCAR stock car is on the fourth floor.

Everything Coca-Cola really should be named "A Few Things Coca-Cola." The small retail outlet has collectibles, free photo ops, and a soda fountain where you can taste 16 Coke products from around the world ($7), but it's a pale vestige of Coke's ambitious marketing ploy, à la M&M's World, that opened in 1997 and closed in 2000. The giant green Coke bottle facade, however, attracts pedestrians into the mall.

Bodies . . . the Exhibition and *Titanic* Artifacts

Although they are tastefully and

respectfully presented, the dissected humans at Bodies . . . the Exhibition (Luxor, 3900 Las Vegas Blvd. S., 702/262-4400 or 800/557-7428, daily 10am-10pm, adults $32, over age 64 $30, age 4-12 $24, under age 4 free) still have the creepy factor. That uneasiness quickly gives way to wonder and interest as visitors examine 13 full-body specimens, carefully preserved to reveal bone structure and muscular, circulatory, respiratory, and other systems. Other system and organ displays drive home the importance of a healthy lifestyle, with structures showing the damage caused by overeating, alcohol consumption, and sedentary lifestyle. Perhaps the most sobering exhibit is the side-by-side comparisons of healthy and smoke-damaged lungs. A draped-off area contains fetal specimens, showing prenatal development and birth defects.

Luxor also hosts the 300 less surreal but just as poignant artifacts and reproductions commemorating the 1912 sinking of the *Titanic* (3900 Las Vegas Blvd. S., 702/262-4400 or 800/557-7428, daily 10am-10pm, adults $32, over age 64 $30, ages 4-12 $24, under age 4 free). The 15-ton rusting hunk of the ship's hull is the biggest artifact on display; it not only drives home the *Titanic*'s scale but also helps transport visitors back to that cold April morning a century ago. A replica of the *Titanic*'s grand staircase—featured prominently in the 1997 film with Leonardo DiCaprio and Kate Winslet—testifies to the ship's opulence, but it is the passengers' personal effects (a pipe, luggage, an unopened bottle of champagne) and recreated first-class and third-class cabins that provide some of the most heartbreaking discoveries. The individual stories come to life as each patron is given the identity of one of the ship's passengers. At the end of tour they find out the passenger's fate.

Shark Reef

Just when you thought it was safe to visit Las Vegas . . . this 1.6-million-gallon habitat proves not all the sharks in town prowl the poker rooms. Shark Reef (Mandalay Bay, 3950 Las Vegas Blvd. S., 702/632-4555, Sun.-Thurs. 10am-8pm, Fri.-Sat. 10am-10pm, adults $18, ages 5-12 $12, under age 5 free) is home to 2,000 animals—almost all predators. Transparent walkthrough tubes and a sinking-ship observation deck allow terrific views, bringing visitors nearly face to face with some of the most fearsome creatures in the world. In addition to 15 species of sharks, guests can view a sand tiger shark, whose mouth is so crammed with razor-sharp teeth that it doesn't fully close. You'll also find golden crocodiles, moray eels, piranhas, giant octopuses, the venomous lion fish, stingrays, jellyfish, water monitors, and the fresh-from-your-nightmares eight-foot-long Komodo dragon.

Mandalay Bay guests with dive certification can dive in the 22-foot-deep shipwreck exhibit at the reef. Commune with eight-foot nurse sharks as well as reef sharks, zebra sharks, rays, sawfish, and other denizens of the deep. Scuba excursions (Tues., Thurs., and Sat.-Sun., age 18 and over, $650) include 3-4 hours underwater, a guided aquarium tour, a video, and admission for up to four guests. Wearing chain mail is required.

Off the Strip
★ Las Vegas Springs Preserve

The Las Vegas Springs Preserve (333 S. Valley View Blvd., 702/822-7700, daily 10am-6pm, adults $19, students and over age 64 $17, ages 5-17 $11, free under age 5) is where Las Vegas began, at least from a Eurocentric viewpoint. More than 100 years ago, the first nonnatives in the Las Vegas Valley—Mormon missionaries from Salt Lake City—stumbled on this clear artesian spring. Of course, the native Paiute and Pueblo people knew about the springs and exploited them millennia before the Mormons arrived. You can see examples of their tools, pottery, and houses at the site, now a 180-acre monument to environmental steward-ship, historic preservation, and geographic discovery. The preserve is home to lizards, rabbits, foxes, scorpions, bats, and more. The nature-minded will love the cactus, rose, and herb gardens, and there's even an occasional cooking demonstration using the desert-friendly fruits, vegetables, and herbs grown here.

Las Vegas has become a leader in water conservation, alternative energy, and other environmentally friendly policies. The results of these efforts and tips on how everyone can reduce their carbon footprint are found in the Sustainability Gallery.

Nevada State Museum

Visitors can spend hours studying Mojave and Spring Mountains ecology, southern Nevada history, and local art at the Nevada State Museum (309 S. Valley View Blvd., 702/486-5205, Thurs.-Mon. 10am-6pm, $19, included in admission to the Springs Preserve). Permanent exhibits on the 13,000-square-foot floor describe southern Nevada's role in warfare and atomic weaponry and include skeletons of a Columbian mammoth, which roamed the Nevada deserts 20,000 years ago, and the ichthyosaur, a whalelike remnant of the Triassic Period. The "Nevada from Dusk to Dawn" exhibit explores the nocturnal lives of the area's animal species. The Cahlan Research Library houses Clark County naturalization and Civil Defense records, among other treasures.

★ Atomic Testing Museum

Kids might not think it's da bomb, but if you were part of the "duck and cover" generation, the Atomic Testing Museum (755 E. Flamingo Rd., 702/794-5161, Mon.-Sat. 10am-5pm, Sun. noon-5pm, adults $12, military, over age 64, ages 7-17, and students $9, under age 7 free) provides plenty to spark your memories of the Cold War. Las Vegas embraced its position as ground zero in the development of the nation's atomic and nuclear

deterrents after World War II. Business leaders welcomed defense contractors to town, and casinos hosted bomb-watching parties as nukes were detonated at the Nevada Test Site, a huge swath of desert 65 miles away. One ingenious marketer promoted the Miss Atomic Bomb beauty pageant in an era when patriotism overcame concerns about radiation.

The museum presents atomic history without bias, walking a fine line between appreciation of the work of nuclear scientists, politicians, and the military and the catastrophic consequences their activities and decisions could have wrought. The museum's best permanent feature is a short video in the Ground Zero Theatre, a multimedia showing of an actual atomic explosion. The theater, a replica of an observation bunker, is rigged for motion, sound, and rushing air.

One gallery helps visitors put atomic energy milestones in historic perspective along with the age's impact on 1950s and 1960s pop culture. The Today and Tomorrow Gallery examines the artifacts associated with explosives, war, and atomic energy, including a section of I-beam from the World Trade Center. Just as relevant today are the lectures and traveling exhibits that the museum hosts. A recent offering was *Journey through Japan,* a look at the postwar culture and development of the only nation to be attacked with atomic weapons.

Computer simulators, high-speed photographs, Geiger counters, and other testing and safety equipment along with first-person accounts add to the museum's visit-worthiness.

Marjorie Barrick Museum of Natural History

The museum and the adjacent Donald H. Baepler Xeric Garden (4505 S. Maryland Pkwy., 702/895-3381, Mon.-Fri. 8am-4:45pm, Sat. 10am-2pm, donation), on the University of Nevada, Las Vegas (UNLV) campus, are good places to bone up on local flora, fauna, and artifacts. First, study the local flora in the arboretum outside the museum entrance, and then step inside for the fauna: small rodents, big snakes, lizards, tortoises, Gila monsters, iguanas, chuckwallas, geckos, spiders, beetles, and cockroaches.

Other displays are full of Native American baskets, kachinas, masks, weaving, pottery, and jewelry from the desert Southwest and Latin America, including Mexican dance masks and traditional Guatemalan textiles.

To find the museum and garden, drive onto the UNLV campus on Harmon Street and follow it around to the right, then turn left into the museum parking lot.

Entertainment

Headliners and Production Shows

Production shows are classic Las Vegas-style entertainment, the kind that most people identify with the Entertainment Capital of the World. An American version of French burlesque, the Las Vegas production show has been gracing various stages around town since the late 1950s and usually includes a magic act, acrobats, jugglers, daredevils, and maybe an animal act. The Cirque du Soleil franchise and *Jubilee!* keep the tradition alive, but other variety shows have given way to more one-dimensional, specialized productions of superstar imitators, sexy song-and-dance reviews, and female impersonators. Most of these are large-budget, skillfully produced and presented extravaganzas, and they are highly entertaining diversions.

As Las Vegas has grown into a sophisticated metropolis, with gourmet restaurants, trendy boutiques, and glittering nightlife, it has also attracted Broadway productions to compete with the superstar singers that helped launch the town's legendary status.

Since they're so expensive to produce, the big shows are fairly reliable, and you can count on them being around for the life of this edition. They do change on occasion; the smaller shows come and go with some frequency, but unless a show bombs and is gone in the first few weeks, it'll usually be around for at least a year. All this big-time entertainment is centered, of course, around Las Vegas's casino resorts, with the occasional concert at the Thomas & Mack Center on the UNLV campus.

Blue Man Group

Bald, blue, and silent (save for homemade PVC musical instruments), Blue Man Group (Venetian, 3355 Las Vegas Blvd. S., 702/414-9000 or 800/258-3626, daily 7pm and 10pm, $65-149) was one of the hottest things to hit the Strip when it debuted at Luxor in 2000 after successful versions in New York, Boston, and Chicago. It continues to wow audiences with its thought-provoking, quirkily hilarious gags and percussion performances. It is part street performance, part slapstick, and all fun.

Carrot Top

With fresh observational humor, outrageous props, and flaming orange hair, Scott Thompson stands alone as the only true full-time headlining stand-up comic in Las Vegas. He's also better known as Carrot Top (Luxor, 3900 Las Vegas Blvd. S., 702/262-4400 or 800/557-7428, Mon. and Wed.-Fri. 8:30pm, $55-66). His rapid-fire, stream-of-consciousness delivery ricochets from sex-aid props and poop jokes to current events, pop culture, and social injustice, making him the thinking person's class clown.

Chippendales

With all the jiggle-and-tease shows on the Strip, Chippendales (Rio, 3700 W. Flamingo Rd., 702/777-2782, Sun.-Wed. 9pm, Thurs.-Sat. 9pm and 11pm, $50-73) delivers a little gender equity. Tight jeans and rippled abs bumping and grinding with their female admirers may be the main attraction, but there is a fairly strict hands-off policy. The boys dance their way through sultry and playful renditions of "It's Raining Men" and other tunes with similar themes.

Donny and Marie

A little bit country, a little bit rock and roll, Donny and Marie Osmond (Flamingo, 3555 Las Vegas Blvd. S., 702/733-3333, Tues.-Sat. 7:30pm, $104-152) manage a bit of hip-hop and soul as well, as they hurl affectionate putdowns at each other between musical numbers. The most famous members of the talented family perform their solo hits, such as Donny's "Puppy Love" and Marie's "Paper Roses" along with perfect-harmony duets while their faux sibling rivalry comes through with good-natured ribbing.

Terry Fator

America's Got Talent champion Terry Fator (Mirage, 3400 Las Vegas Blvd. S., 702/792-7777 or 800/963-9634, Mon.-Thurs. 8pm, $59-129) combines two disparate skills—ventriloquism and impersonation—to channel Elvis, Garth Brooks, Lady Gaga and others. Backed by a live band, Fator sings and trades one-liners with his foam rubber friends. The comedy is fresh, the impressions spot-on, and the ventriloquism accomplished with nary a lip quiver.

Matt Goss

A three-year deal he signed in 2010 means Matt Goss (Caesars Palace, 3570 Las Vegas Blvd. S., 800/745-3000, Fri.-Sat. 10pm, $40-95) will be delivering his selections from the great American songbook for some time to come. Backed by a swingin' nine-piece band and the requisite sexy dancers, Goss, in fedora and bow tie, brings his own style to standards like "I've Got the World on a String," "Luck Be a Lady," and other Rat Pack favorites.

Jersey Boys

The rise of Frankie Valli and the Four Seasons from street-corner doo-woppers to superstars gets the full Broadway treatment in *Jersey Boys* (Paris, 3655 Las Vegas Blvd. S., 877/242-6753, Sun. and Wed.-Fri. 7pm, Tues. 6:30pm and 9:30pm, Sat. 8:15pm, $53-244). *Jersey Boys* is the true story of the falsetto-warbling Valli and his bandmates. Terrific sets and lighting create the mood, alternating from the grittiness of the Newark streets to the flash of the concert stage. Remember, it's the story of inner-city teens in the 1950s, so be prepared for more than a few F-bombs in the dialogue.

★ Jubilee!

What used to be the last of old-style Vegas variety shows, *Jubilee!* (Bally's, 3645 Las Vegas Blvd. S., 702/777-2782 or 855/234-7469, Thurs. 7pm, Sun.-Wed. 7pm and 10pm, Sat. 10pm, $71-115) morphed into showgirl (and showboy) heaven. Not that there's anything wrong with dozens of the statuesque, feathered, rhinestoned (not to mention, topless) beauties performing lavishly choreographed production routines. But we miss the vaudevillian acrobats, contortionists, aerialists, jugglers, and other specialty acts. Complicated production numbers with intricate dance steps and nearly 100 performers on the 150-foot stage give the showgirls appropriate backdrops for strutting their stuff, and the climactic sinking of the *Titanic* is a real show-stopper.

Kà

Cirque du Soleil's *Kà* (MGM Grand, 3799 Las Vegas Blvd. S., 702/531-3826 or 800/929-1111, Tues.-Sat. 7pm and 9:30pm, $69-150) explores the yin and yang of life through the story of two twins' journey to meet their shared fate. Martial arts, acrobatics, plenty of flashy pyrotechnics, and lavish sets and costumes bring cinematic drama to the variety-show acts. The show's title was inspired by the ancient Egyptian *Ka* belief, in which every human has a spiritual duplicate.

Legends in Concert
The best of the celebrity impersonator shows, *Legends in Concert* (3555 Las Vegas Blvd. S., 702/777-7776 or 855/234-7469, Sat.-Mon. and Wed.-Thurs. 4pm and 9:30pm, Tues. 9:30pm, Sun. 7:30pm and 9:30pm, $50-82), brings out the "stars" in rapid-fire succession. Madonna barely finishes striking a pose before the Blues Brothers hit the stage. You'll see Elvis, of course, and five or six other acts from Britney, Cher, and Gaga to Garth, Reba, and Dolly. A Vegas fixture for 25 years, *Legends* is truly legendary.

Le Rêve
All the spectacle we've come to expect from the creative geniuses behind Cirque du Soleil is present in this stream-of-unconsciousness known as *Le Rêve* (Wynn, 3131 Las Vegas Blvd. S., 702/770-WYNN—702/770-9966 or 888/320-7110, Fri.-Tues. 7pm and 9:30pm, $105-159). The loose concept is a romantically conflicted woman's fevered dream (*rêve* in French). Some 80 perfectly sculpted specimens of human athleticism and beauty cavort, flip, swim, and show off their muscles around a huge aquatic stage. More than 2,000 guests fill the theater in the round, with seats all within 50 feet; those in the first couple of rows are in the "splash zone." Clowns and acrobats complete the package.

★ LOVE
For Beatles fans visiting Las Vegas, all you need is *LOVE* (Mirage, 3400 Las Vegas Blvd. S., 702/792-7777 or 800/963-9634, Thurs.-Mon. 7pm and 9:30pm, $79-180). This Cirque du Soleil-produced trip down Penny Lane features dancers, aerial acrobats, and other performers interpreting the Fab Four's lyrics and recordings. With the breathtaking visual artistry of Cirque du Soleil and a custom sound-scape using the original master tapes from Abbey Road Studios, John, Paul, George, and Ringo have never looked or sounded so good.

Million Dollar Quartet
A surprisingly strong storyline augments the Sun Records catalog in *Million Dollar Quartet* (Harrah's, 3475 Las Vegas Blvd. S., 702/777-2782 or 855/234-7469, Tues.-Wed. and Fri. 7pm, Mon. and Thurs. 5:30pm and 8pm, $63-87), a chronicle of the world's coolest jam session. The musical tells the events of December 4, 1956, when budding superstars Elvis Presley and Johnny Cash popped in to studio to say hello to Sun owner Sam Phillips. Carl Perkins happened to be recording at the time, and Phillips was augmenting the orchestration with an unknown pianist named Jerry Lee Lewis.

Mystère
At first glance, Cirque du Soleil production *Mystère* (Treasure Island, 3300 Las Vegas Blvd. S., 702/894-7722 or 800/392-1999, Sat.-Wed. 7pm and 9:30pm, $69-119) is like a circus. But it also plays on other performance archetypes, including classical Greek theater, Kabuki, athletic prowess, and surrealism. The first Cirque show in Las Vegas, *Mystère* continues to dazzle audiences with its revelations of life's mysteries.

O
Bellagio likes to do everything bigger, better, and more extravagant, and *O* (Bellagio, 3600 Las Vegas Blvd. S., 702/693-7722 or 888/488-7111, Wed.-Sun. 7:30pm and 10pm, $98-155) is no exception. This Vegas Cirque du Soleil incarnation involves a $90 million set, 80 artists, and a 1.5-million-gallon pool of water. The title comes from the French word for water, *eau,* pronounced like the letter *O* in English. The production involves both terrestrial and aquatic feats of human artistry, athleticism, and comedy. It truly must be seen to be believed.

Penn & Teller

The oddball comedy magicians Penn & Teller (Rio, 3700 W. Flamingo Rd., 866/983-4279, Sat.-Wed. 9pm, $83-117) have a way of making audiences feel special. Seemingly breaking the magicians' code, they reveal the preparation and sleight-of-hand involved in performing tricks. The hitch is that even when forewarned, observers still often can't catch on. And once they do, the verbose Penn and silent Teller add a wrinkle no one expects.

Britney Spears: *Piece of Me*

Pop superstar Britney Spears (Planet Hollywood, 3667 Las Vegas Blvd. S., 866/919-7472, Wed. and Fri.-Sun. 9pm, $77-344) flaunts her toned frame while performing sexy and energetic renditions of her hits and new material. With her patented dance moves and choreography incorporating fly systems, fire, mirrors, and barely-there costumes, Britney reinforces her diva status. If you want to see her, you'll have to hurry; the rumor is she'll retire when her Planet Hollywood run ends in 2015.

Tony n' Tina's Wedding

Feuding future in-laws, a drunken priest, a libidinous nun, and a whole flock of black sheep can't keep Tony and Tina from finding wedded bliss in *Tony n' Tina's Wedding* (Bally's, 3645 Las Vegas Blvd. S., 702/777-2782, 855/234-7469, Mon., Wed., and Fri.-Sat. 6pm, $109-149). Or can they? You play the role of a wedding guest, sitting among the actors, where you learn where the family skeletons are hidden and the bodies are buried. Will you play the peacemaker, or stir up the jealousies and hidden agendas among the family members? Each show is different, based on the audience reaction. So keep your ears peeled; you just might pick up the juiciest gossip between the lasagna and the cannoli.

Tournament of Kings

Pound on the table with your goblet and let loose a hearty "huzzah!" to cheer your king to victory over the other nation's regents at the *Tournament of Kings* (Excalibur, 3580 Las Vegas Blvd. S., 702/597-7600, Mon. and Fri. 6pm, Wed.-Thurs. and Sat.-Sun. 6pm and 8:30pm, $59). Each section of the equestrian theater rallies under separate banners as their hero participates in jousts, sword fights, riding contests and lusty-maid flirting at this festival hosted by King Arthur and Merlin. A regal feast, served medieval style (that is, without utensils), starts with a tureen of dragon's blood (tomato soup). But just as the frivolity hits its climax, an evil lord appears to wreak havoc. Can the kings and Merlin's magic save the day? One of the best family shows in Las Vegas.

Zumanity

Cirque du Soleil seems to have succumbed to the titillation craze with the strange melding of sexuality, athleticism, and comedy that is *Zumanity* (New York New York, 3790 Las Vegas Blvd. S., 866/606-7111, Fri.-Tues. 7:30pm and 10pm, $69-129). The cabaret-style show makes no pretense of storyline, but instead takes audience members through a succession of sexual and topless fantasies—French maids, schoolgirls, and light autoerotic S&M.

Showroom and Lounge Acts

Showrooms are another Las Vegas institution, with most hotels providing live entertainment—usually magic, comedy, or tributes to the big stars who played or are playing the big rooms and theaters under the same roofs.

The Vegas lounge act is the butt of a few jokes, but they offer some of the best entertainment values in town—a night's entertainment for the price of a few drinks and a small cover charge. Every hotel in Las Vegas worth its salt has a lounge, and the acts change often enough to make them hangouts for locals. These acts are listed in the free entertainment magazines and the *Las Vegas Review-Journal*'s helpful website, but unless you're familiar with the performers, it's the luck of the draw: They list only the entertainer's name, venue, and showtimes.

The Rat Pack Is Back

Relive the golden era when Frank, Dean, Sammy, and Joey ruled the Strip with *The Rat Pack Is Back* (Rio, 3700 W. Flamingo Rd., 702/777-2782, Wed.-Mon. 6:30pm, $66-134). Watch Sinatra try to make it through *Luck Be a Lady* amid the others' sophomoric antics. Frank plays right along, pretending to rule his crew with an iron fist, as the crew treats him with the mock deference the Chairman of the Board deserves.

The King **Starring Trent Carlini**

Crowned *The Next Big Thing* on the ABC TV contest, Trent Carlini (Westgate, 3000 Paradise Rd., 866/983-4279, Wed.-Mon. 8pm, $63-84) is the best of the 245 registered Elvis impersonators in town, combining a strong resemblance to the King with pitch-perfect singing. His show focuses on the songs Presley made famous during his film career.

Mac King Comedy Magic

The quality of afternoon shows in Las Vegas is spotty at best, but Mac King Comedy Magic (Harrah's, 3475 Las Vegas Blvd. S., 866/983-4279, Tues.-Sat. 1pm and 3pm, $39) fits the bill for talent and affordability. King's routine is clean both technically and content-wise. With a plaid suit, good manners, and a silly grin, he cuts a nerdy figure, but his tricks and banter are skewed enough to make even the most jaded teenager laugh.

Human Nature: The Motown Show

Blue-eyed soul gets the Down Under treatment with the exhaustingly titled *Smokey Robinson Presents Human Nature: The Motown Show* (Venetian, 3355 Las Vegas Blvd. S., 702/414-9000, Sun.-Fri. 7pm, $42-117). Four clean-cut, well-dressed Aussies, backed by a small live band, channel The Temptations, The Miracles, and others with enough verve and coordinated dance moves to make Robinson a fan.

Divas Las Vegas

Veteran female impersonator Frank Marino has been headlining on the Strip for 25 years, and he still looks good—with or without eye shadow and falsies. Marino stars as emcee Joan Rivers, leading fellow impersonators who lip-synch their way through cheeky renditions of tunes by Lady Gaga, Liza Minnelli, Cher, Madonna, and others in *Divas Las Vegas* (Linq, 3535 Las Vegas Blvd. S., 702/777-2782 or 866/574-3851, Sat.-Thurs. 9:30pm, $55-96).

Vinnie Favorito

Vinnie Favorito (Flamingo, 3555 Las Vegas Blvd. S., 702/885-1451, daily 8pm, $69-75) is not impressed, and he'll let you know it. Whatever your profession, level of education, athletic achievement, or other worthy attribute, Favorito will turn it into an instrument of shame. Working with no set material, Favorito is reminiscent of Don Rickles, mingling with and interviewing audience members to find fodder for his quick wit.

Gordie Brown

A terrific song stylist in his own right, Gordie Brown (Golden Nugget, 129 E. Fremont St., 866/983-4279, Tues.-Sat. 7:30pm, $37-75) is the thinking person's singing impressionist. Using his targets' peccadilloes as fodder for his song parodies, Brown pokes serious fun with a surgeon's precision. Props, mannerisms, and absurd vignettes incorporating several celebrity voices at once add to the madcap fun.

Comedy

Comedy in Las Vegas has undergone a shift in recent years. Nearly gone are the days of top-name comedians as resident headliners. Those gigs increasingly go to singers and production shows. In fact, Carrot Top, at the Luxor, is about the only long-term funnyman left. However, A-list funny females have a new stage, Lipshtick (Venetian, 3355 Las Vegas Blvd. S., 866/641-7469, Fri. 10pm, Sat. 7:30pm, $54-118), which hosts the likes of Lisa Lampanelli, Joy Behar, Wendy Williams, and Roseanne Barr. The other biggies—Jay Leno, Daniel Tosh, and Ron White, among others—still make regular appearances in the major showrooms on big Vegas weekends at venues such as Aces of Comedy at the Mirage (3400 Las Vegas Blvd. S., 702/791-7111, Fri. 10pm, Sat. 8pm, $85-110). But most of the yuks nowadays come from the talented youngsters toiling in the comedy club trenches.

The journeymen and up-and-coming have half a dozen places to land gigs when they're in town. Among the best are The Improv at Harrah's (3475 Las Vegas Blvd. S., 702/777-2782, Tues.-Sun. 8:30pm and 10:30pm, $37-56), Brad Garrett's Comedy Club at the MGM Grand (3799 Las Vegas Blvd. S., 888/646-1203, daily 8pm, $46-68, plus $20 when Garrett performs), and the Laugh Factory at the Tropicana (801 Las Vegas Blvd. S., 866/983-4279, daily 8:30pm and 10:30pm, $38-49).

Magic

Magic shows are nearly as ubiquitous as comedy, with the more accomplished, such as Penn & Teller, Chris Angel, and David Copperfield (MGM Grand, 3799 Las Vegas Blvd. S., 866/983-4279, Sun.-Fri. 7pm and 9:30pm, Sun. 4pm, 7pm, and 9:30pm, $98) playing long-term gigs in their own showrooms. The best smaller-scale shows include Illusions Starring Jan Rouven at the Riviera (2901 Las Vegas Blvd. S., 855/468-6748, Sat.-Thurs. 7pm, $59-99), with its death-defying illusions involving knives and water chambers; and the budget-conscious Laughternoon (The D, 301 Fremont St., 702/388-2400, daily 4pm, $25), where Adam London turns his unhealthy obsession with duckies into comedy sleight-of-hand.

Live Music

With all the entertainment that casinos have to offer—and the budgets to bring in the best—there's some surprising talent lurking in the dives, meat markets, and neighborhood pubs around Las Vegas. Locals who don't want to deal with the hassles of a trip to the Strip and visitors whose musical tastes don't match the often-mainstream pop-rock-country genre of the resort lounges might find a gem or two by venturing away from the neon.

The newest, best, and most convenient venue for visitors, Brooklyn Bowl (Linq Promenade, 3545 Las Vegas Blvd. S., Suite 22, 702/862-2695, Mon.-Fri. 5pm-late, Sat.-Sun. noon-late) replicates its successful New York City formula with 32 lanes, comfortable couches, beer, and big-name groups sprinkled among the party band lineup. Elvis Costello, Wu-Tang Clan, Jane's Addiction, and Cake are among the notables that have played the Brooklyn. Showtimes range from noon to midnight, often with several acts slated through the day.

With more than 20,000 square feet of space and a 2,500-square-foot dance floor, Stoney's Rockin' Country (6611 Las Vegas Blvd. S., Suite 300, 702/435-2855, Wed.-Sat. 7pm-2am) could almost *be* its own country. It is honky-tonk on a grand scale, with a mechanical bull and line-dancing lessons. Muddy Waters, Etta James, B. B. King, and even Mick Jagger have graced the stage at the recently re-opened Sand Dollar (3355 Spring Mountain Rd., 312/515-1389), where blue-collar blues rule. Bands start around 10pm weekdays, 7:30pm weekends. The people your mama warned you about hang out at the never-a-cover-charge Double Down Saloon (4640 Paradise Rd., 702/791-5775), drinking to excess and thrashing to the punk, ska, and psychobilly bands on stage.

The Arts

With so much plastic, neon, and reproduction statuary around town, it's easy to accuse Las Vegas of being a soulless, cultureless wasteland, and many have. But Las Vegans don't live in casino hotels and eat every meal in the buffet. We don't all make our living as dealers and cocktail waitresses. Las Vegas, like most others, is a city built of communities. So why shouldn't Las Vegas enjoy and foster the arts? As home to an urban university and many profitable businesses just itching to prove their corporate citizenry, southern Nevada's arts are as viable as any city of comparable size in the country.

The local performing arts are thriving, thanks to the 2012 construction of the Smith Center for the Performing Arts (361 Symphony Park Ave., 702/749-2012, www.thesmithcenter.com), a major cog in the revitalization of downtown, along with the development of 61 acres of former Union Pacific Railroad land the city has been working to turn into a pedestrian-friendly showplace. It is home to the Las Vegas Philharmonic, the Nevada Ballet Theatre, the Cabaret Jazz series, local and school performances and classes, and the best theatrical touring companies.

Classical Music

The Las Vegas Philharmonic (702/258-5438, http://lvphil.org) presents a full schedule of pops, masterworks, holiday, and youth performances at the Smith Center. The Phil also works with the local school district to develop music education classes.

Ballet

With a 36,000-square-foot training facility, Nevada Ballet Theatre (702/243-2623, www.nevadaballet.com) trains hundreds of aspiring ballerinas age 18 months through adults and provides practice and performance space for its professional company. The company presents classical and contemporary performances throughout the year at the Smith Center. The Las Vegas Ballet Company (702/240-3263, www.lasvegasballet.org) was founded by former Nevada Ballet Theatre principal dancers as a performance outlet for students at their ballet and modern dance academy.

Theater

Theater abounds in Las Vegas, with various troupes staging mainstream plays, musical comedy, and experimental productions. Las Vegas Little Theatre (3920 Schiff Dr., 702/362-7996, www.lvlt.org), the town's oldest community troupe, performs mostly mainstream shows in its Mainstage series and takes a few more chances on productions in its Black Box theater. Cockroach Theatre Company (1025 S. 1st St., 702/818-3422, www.cockroachtheare.com) stages mostly serious productions (think Camus, Albee, and Miller) in the Art Square Theater in the Arts District.

The highest-quality acting and production values can be found at the University of Nevada, Las Vegas, Performing Arts Center (4505 S. Maryland Pkwy., 702/895-ARTS—702/895-2787, http://pac.unlv.edu), comprising the Artemus Ham Concert Hall, the Judy Bayley Theater, and the Alta Ham Black Box Theater. The Nevada Conservatory Theatre, the university's troupe of advanced students and visiting professional actors, performs fall-spring. Shows run from the farcical to the poignant; *My Children! My Africa* and *The 25th Annual Putnam County Spelling Bee* bookend the 2014-2015 season.

Guests become witnesses, sleuths, and even suspects in Marriage Can Be Murder (The D, 301 Fremont St., 702/388-2400, daily 6:15pm, $65) interactive dinner theater. Soon the bodies start piling up between the one-liners and slapstick. Dig out your deerstalker and magnifying glass and help catch that killer.

Visual Art

Outside the downtown arts district and the fabulous art collections amassed and displayed by Steve Wynn and other casino magnates, the **Donna Beam Fine Art Gallery** at UNLV (4505 S. Maryland Pkwy., 702/895-3893, www.unlv.edu/donnabeamgallery, Mon.-Fri. 9am-5pm, Sat. 10am-2pm, free) hosts exhibitions by nationally and internationally known painters, sculptors, designers, potters, and other visual artists. In addition to helping visitors enhance their critical thinking and aesthetic sensitivity, the exhibits teach UNLV students the skills needed in gallery management.

Rides and Games
Stratosphere Tower

Daredevils will delight in the vertigo-inducing thrill rides on the observation deck at the **Stratosphere Tower** (200 Las Vegas Blvd. S., 702/380-7711, Sun.-Thurs. 10am-1am, Fri.-Sat. 10am-2am, $15-120). The newest ride, Sky Jump Las Vegas, invites the daring to plunge into space for a 15-second free fall. Angled guide wires keep jumpers on target and ease them to gentle landings. This skydive without a parachute costs $120. The other rides are 100-story-high variations on traditional thrill rides: The Big Shot is a sort of 15-person reverse bungee jump; X-Scream sends riders on a gentle (at first) roll off the edge, leaving them suspended over Las Vegas Boulevard; Insanity's giant arms swing over the edge, tilting to suspend riders nearly horizontally. These attractions are $15 each, plus a charge just to ride the elevator to the top of the tower (adults $20, children $12, seniors and Nevada residents $12). Multiple-ride packages and all-day passes are available but don't include the Sky Jump.

SlotZilla

For an up-close and high-speed view of the Fremont Street Experience canopy and the iconic casino signs, take a zoom on **SlotZilla** (425 Fremont St., 702/678-5780 or 844/947-8342, Sun.-Thurs. noon-midnight, Fri.-Sat. noon-2am, $20-30), a 1,750-foot-long zip line that takes off from a the world's largest slot machine (only in Vegas, right?). Riders are launched horizontally, Superman-style, for a 40-mph slide. For the less adventurous, SlotZilla also operates a lower, slower, half-as-long version.

Adventuredome

Behind Circus Circus, the **Adventuredome Theme Park** (2880 Las Vegas Blvd. S., 702/794-3939, summer daily 10am-midnight, during the school year daily 10am-9pm, over 48 inches tall $30, under 48 inches $17) houses two roller coasters, a 4-D motion simulator, laser tag, and vertigo-inducing amusements machines—all inside a pink plastic shell. The main teen and adult attractions are the coasters—El Loco and Canyon Blaster, the largest indoor coaster in the world with speeds up to 55 mph, which is pretty rough. The five-acre fun park can host birthday parties. The all-day passes are a definite bargain over individual ride prices, but carnival games, food vendors, and special rides and games not included in the pass give parents extra chances to spend money. It's not the Magic Kingdom, but it has rides to satisfy all ages and bravery levels. Besides, Las Vegas is supposed to be the *adult* Disneyland.

Wet 'n' Wild

With rides conjuring Las Vegas, the desert, and the Southwest, **Wet 'n' Wild** (7055 Fort Apache Rd., 702/979-1600, hours vary, closed weekdays during the school year, $40, discounts for seniors, guests under 42 inches tall, and after 4pm) provides a welcome respite from the dry heat of southern Nevada. Challenge the Royal Flush Extreme, which whisks riders through a steep pipe before swirling them around a simulated porcelain commode and down the tube. The water park boasts 11 rides of varying terror levels, along with a Kiddie Cove. Guests must be over 42 inches tall to enjoy all the rides.

Indy and NASCAR Driving

Calling all gearheads! If you're ready to take the wheel of a 600-hp stock car, check out the **Richard Petty Driving Experience** (Las Vegas Motor Speedway, 7000 Las Vegas Blvd. N., 800/ BE-PETTY—800/237-3889, days and times vary, $109-2,699). The "Rookie Experience" ($499) lets NASCAR wannabes put the stock car through its paces for eight laps around the 1.5-mile tri-oval after extensive in-car and on-track safety training. Participants also receive a lap-by-lap breakdown of their run, transportation to and from the Strip, and a tour of the Driving Experience Race Shop. Even more intense—and more expensive—experiences, with more laps and more in-depth instruction, are available. To feel the thrill without the responsibility, opt for the three-lap ride-along ($109) in a two-seat stock car with a professional driver at the wheel.

Sports
Golf

With its climate, endless sunshine, and vacation destination status, it's no wonder that Las Vegas is home to more than 40 golf courses. Virtually all are eminently playable and fair, although the dry heat makes the greens fast and the city's valley location can make for some havoc-wreaking winds in the spring. Las Vegas courses, especially in recent years, have removed extraneous water-loving landscaping, opting for xeriscape and desert landscape, irrigating the fairways and greens with reclaimed water. Greens fees and amenities range from affordable municipal-type courses to some of the most exclusive country clubs anywhere. The following is a selective list in each budget category.

The only course open to the public on the Strip is **Bali Hai** (5160 Las Vegas Blvd. S., 888/427-6678, $150-199), next to Mandalay Bay on the south end of casino row. The South Pacific theme includes lots of lush green tropical foliage, deep azure ponds, and black volcanic outcroppings. A handful of long par-4s are fully capable of making a disaster of your scorecard even before you reach the par-3 sphincter-clenching 16th. Not only does it play to an island green, it comes with a built-in gallery where you can enjoy your discomfort while dining on Bali Hai's restaurant patio.

There's plenty of water to contend with at **Siena Golf Club** (10575 Siena Monte Ave., 702/341-9200 or 888/689-6469, $59-139). Six small lakes, deep fairway bunkers, and desert scrub provide significant challenges off the tee, but five sets of tee boxes even things out for shorter hitters. The large, fairly flat greens are fair and readable. A perfect example of many courses' move toward more ecofriendly design, **Painted Desert** (5555 Painted Mirage Rd., 702/645-2570, $26-75) uses cacti, mesquites, and other desert plants to separate its links-style fairways. The 6,323-yard, par-72 course isn't especially challenging, especially if you're straight off the tee, making it a good choice for getting back to the fundamentals. Bring plenty of balls when you accept the challenge at **Badlands** (9119 Alta Dr., 702/363-0754, $55-155), as you'll routinely be asked to carry beautiful but intimidating desert gullies and ravines full of lush wildflowers and cacti. The three 9-hole layouts do not forgive poor tee shots, and even if you do find your ball, hitting from this rough delivers more punishment for golfer and clubface alike.

Las Vegas Motor Speedway

Home to NASCAR's Sprint Cup and Boyd Gaming 300 Nationwide Series race, the **Las Vegas Motor Speedway** (7000 Las Vegas Blvd. N., 800/644-4444) is a racing omniplex. In addition to the superspeedway, a 1.5-mile tri-oval for NASCAR races, the site also brings in dragsters to its quarter-mile strip; modifieds, late models, bandoleros, legends, bombers, and more to its paved oval; and off-roaders to its half-mile clay oval.

The speedway underwent a multimillion-dollar renovation project between NASCAR Weekends in 2006 and 2007, resulting in an unprecedented interactive fan experience known as the Neon Garage. Located in the speedway's infield, Neon Garage has unique and gourmet concession stands, live entertainment, and the winner's circle. Fans can get up close or watch drivers and crews from bird's-eye perches.

Sadly, IndyCar World Racing discontinued its relationship with LVMS following the horrific crash in 2011 that claimed the life of driver Dan Wheldon.

Boxing and Mixed Martial Arts

Despite many promoters opting for cheaper venues, Las Vegas retains the title as heavyweight boxing champion of the world. Nevada's legalized sports betting, its history, and the facilities at the MGM Grand Garden and Mandalay Bay Events Center make it a natural for the biggest matches.

Many of the casinos that once held mid-level bouts have opted for more lucrative events, meaning fewer chances to see up-and-comers working their way up the ladder for a shot at a minor alphabet-soup belt. Still, fight fans can find a card pretty much every month from March to October at either the Hard Rock, Sam's Town, Sunset Station, Palms, or other midsize arena or showroom. The fighters are hungry, the matches are entertaining, and the cost is low, with tickets priced $25-100.

For the megafights, however, expect to dole out big bucks to get inside the premier venues. The "cheap" seats at MGM and Mandalay Bay often cost a car payment and require the Hubble telescope to see any action. Ringside seats require

a mortgage payment. Check the venues' websites for tickets.

Mixed martial arts continues to grow in popularity, with MGM and Mandalay Bay hosting UFC title fights about every other month. For those who prefer sanctioned bar fights, Big Knockout Boxing made its debut in Vegas in 2014. This take on the fight game takes place in a 17-foot-diameter circle; no ropes, no corners, no place to hide. Five or seven two-minute rounds leave precious little time for dancing, grabbing, and point scoring, making the haymaker punch the star of the show.

Accommodations

Choosing Accommodations

Casinos offer both the most opulent hotel accommodations in town and the widest variety of options. See the *Casinos* section for information on these rooms.

If you opt not to stay in a casino, you'll still find plenty of options. Las Vegas boasts more than 100 hotels and 200 motels, but sometimes that makes it harder, not easier, to choose. Keep in mind that most accommodations either sell out or nearly sell out every weekend of the year. Long weekends and holidays, especially New Year's Eve, Valentine's Day, Memorial Day, Fourth of July, Labor Day, and Thanksgiving, along with international holidays such as Cinco de Mayo, Mexican Independence Day, and Chinese New Year, are sold out weeks in advance. Special events such as concerts, title fights, the Super Bowl, the Final Four, NASCAR Weekend, and the National Finals Rodeo are sold out months in advance. Reservations are made for the biggest conventions (Consumer Electronics, Men's Apparel, and so on) a year ahead of time.

There are some minor quiet times, such as the three weeks before Christmas and July-August, when the mercury doesn't drop below 90°F. If you're just coming for the weekend, keep in mind

Grand Canyon Tours from Vegas

Nearly a dozen tour companies relay visitors from Vegas to and through the Grand Canyon via a variety of conveyances—buses, airplanes, helicopters, off-road vehicles, and rafts. Coupons and discounts for online reservation and off-season bookings are plentiful; it is not uncommon to book tours at less than half the rack rates listed here.

Grand Canyon Tours
Grand Canyon Tours (702/655-6060 or 800/2-CANYON—800/222-6966, www.grandcanyontours.com) packs plenty of sightseeing into its bus tours ($180-190). which can include the Grand Canyon Railway or Hualapai Ranch. Helicopter tours ($355-495) cut down the commute, leaving more time at the canyon and allow an earlier return. Choppers skim over Hoover Dam, Lake Mead, the Black Mountains, and the Strip during the 1.5-hour flight. Stops can include the Grand Canyon Skywalk, Grand Canyon West Ranch, and the canyon floor.

Look Tours
Look Tours (4285 N. Rancho Dr., 702/233-1627 or 800/LOOK-TOURS—800/566-5868, www.looktours.com) also offers bus tours (daily 6am-10pm, $165) and an overnight trip via fixed-wing aircraft ($442-512). Do-it-yourselfers can rent an SUV from Look (daily 7am, 8am, or 9am, $170 pp, 2-person minimum) for a leisurely 24-hour exploration of the West Rim.

Maverick Helicopter Tours
Maverick Helicopter Tours (6075 Las Vegas Blvd. S., 702/261-0007 or 888/261-4414, and 1410 Jet Stream Dr., Suite 100, Henderson, 702/405-4300 or 888/261-4414, www.maverickhelicopter.com) shuttles its customers to the canyon via spacious, quiet Eco-Star helicopters (daily 7am-4:30pm, $619) and partners with Pink Jeep Tours for a guided road tour to the West Rim followed by a slow descent to the bottom of the canyon (daily 6am-5pm, $395).

SweeTours
SweeTours (6363 S. Pecos Rd., Suite 106, Las Vegas, 702/456-9200, http://sweetours.com) offers several pacakages ($169-385), which include options for travel by bus, SUV, helicopter, and boat.

that most of the major hotels don't even let you check in on a Saturday night. You can stay Friday and Saturday, but not Saturday alone. It may be easier to find a room Sunday-Thursday, when there aren't any large conventions or sporting events. Almost all the room packages and deep discounts are only available on these days.

Hotels
Center Strip
With a name like Trump (2000 Fashion Show Dr., 702/892-0000 or 866/939-4279, $131-284), you know that no whim will go unfulfilled. Standard rooms open onto an Italian marble entryway leading to floor-to-ceiling windows with the requisite magnificent views. In-room amenities include dual sinks with Italian marble countertops, and 32-inch flat-screen TVs. Feather comforters and Italian linens make for heavenly restfulness. Dining options include the chic DJT steak house and the hip H2(EAU) poolside. The Spa at Trump offers unique packages such as the Body Radiance Salt Scrub ($140).

One of the newest landmarks on the Las Vegas skyline, Platinum (211 E. Flamingo Rd., 702/365-5000 or 877/211-9211, $123-220) treats both guests and the environment with kid gloves. The resort uses the latest technology to reduce its carbon footprint through such measures as low-energy lighting throughout, eco-friendly room thermostats, and motion sensors to turn lights off when restrooms are unoccupied. Suites are an expansive 950 square feet of muted designer furnishings and accents, and they include all modern conveniences, such as high-speed Internet, high-fidelity sound systems, full kitchens, and oversize tubs. **Kilowatt** (daily 6am-2pm, $10-20) with sleek silver decor accented with dark woods, is a feast for the eyes and the palate for breakfast and lunch.

Lower Strip

Feel like royalty at the ★ **Mandarin Oriental Las Vegas** (3752 Las Vegas Blvd. S., 702/590-8888, www.mandarinoriental.com/lasvegas, $295-995), which looks down on the bright lights of the strip from a peaceful remove. A master control panel in each of the modern rooms sets the atmosphere to your liking, controlling the lights, temperature, window curtains, and more. Once everything is set, sink into a warm bath and watch TV on the flat screen embedded in the bath mirror. Another impressive feature is the valet closet, which allows hotel staff to deliver items to your room without entering your unit. The **Mandarin Bar** (888/881-9367, Mon.-Thurs. 4pm-1am, Fri.-Sat. 4pm-2am, Sun. 4pm-11pm) on the 23rd floor offers stunning views of the city skyline. And it's all environmentally friendly, or at least LEED-certified.

Offering sophisticated accommodations and amenities without the hubbub of a rowdy casino, the **Renaissance** (3400 Paradise Rd., 702/784-5700 or 800/750-0980, $120-200) has big, bright, airy standard guest rooms that come complete with triple-sheeted 300-thread-count Egyptian cotton beds with down comforters and duvets, walk-in showers, full tubs, 32-inch flat-panel TVs, a business center, and high-speed Internet. Upper-floor guest rooms overlook the Wynn golf course. The pool and whirlpool are outside, and the concierge can score show tickets and tee times. **Envy Steakhouse** (daily 6:30am-2pm and 5pm-10pm, brunch Sun. 11am-3pm, $30-50) has a few seafood entrées, but the Angus beef gets top billing.

Every guest room is a suite at the **Signature** (45 E. Harmon Ave., 877/612-2121 or 800/452-4520, $160-30) at MGM Grand. Even the junior suite is a roomy 550 square feet and includes a standard king bed, kitchenette, and spa tub. Most of the 1,728 smoke-free guest rooms in the gleaming 40-story tower include private balconies with Strip views, and guests have access to the complimentary 24-hour fitness center, three outdoor pools, a business center, and free wireless Internet throughout the hotel. A gourmet deli and acclaimed room service satisfy noshing needs, and **The Lounge** provides a quiet, intimate spot for discussing business or pleasure over drinks.

The condominium suites at **Desert Rose** (5051 Duke Ellington Way, 702/739-7000 or 888/732-8099, $120-350) are loaded, with new appliances and granite countertops in the kitchen as well as private balconies or patios outside. One-bedroom suites are quite large, at 650 square feet, and sleep four comfortably. Rates vary widely, but depending on your needs and travel dates, you might find a suite deal.

Although it includes a full-service casino and is just steps from the Strip, the draw of the **Tuscany** (255 E. Flamingo Rd., 702/893-8933 or 877/887-2264, $90-180) is the relaxed atmosphere, from its restaurants and lounges to its lagoon pool. The sprawling 27-acre site with footpaths and impeccable landscaping belies its proximity to the rush-rush of the Strip one block west. Dining here is more low-key than at many of Tuscany's neighbors. Although there is a semiformal restaurant, **Tuscany Gardens** (daily 5pm-10pm, $25-35), the casual **Cantina** (Mon.-Thurs. 11am-9:30pm, Fri. 11am-midnight, Sat. 10am-midnight, Sun. 10am-9:30pm, $10-20) and **Marilyn's Café** (daily 24 hours, $8-15) are more in keeping with the resort's métier. That's not to say Tuscany is strictly the purview of fuddy-duddies; the 50,000-square-foot casino has all the games you expect in Las Vegas, and there's entertainment

Tuesday-Saturday in the Piazza Lounge. All suites, the Tuscany's guest rooms boast more than 625 square feet and come with galley kitchens, wet bars, 25-inch TVs, and mini fridges.

Motels
The Strip

Several good-value motels are located on Las Vegas Boulevard South between the Stratosphere and the Riviera; these places are also good to try for weekly rooms with kitchenettes. When the temperature isn't in the triple digits, they're also within walking distance to the Sahara, Riviera, Circus Circus, and the Adventuredome. **Clarion** (305 Convention Center Dr., 702/952-8000, $55-100 d) offers clean doubles.

Motels along the lower Strip, from Bally's below Flamingo Avenue all the way out to the Mandalay Bay at the far south end of the Strip, are well placed to visit all the new big-brand casino resorts but have prices that match the cheaper places north of downtown. The independent motels are hit-and-miss. You're better off sticking with established brands like **Travelodge Las Vegas Strip** (3735 S. Las Vegas Blvd., 702/736-3443, $59-99), which gets a top rating for its reasonable prices; location near the MGM Grand, Luxor, and Mandalay Bay; and little extras like free continental breakfast, newspapers, and a heated swimming pool. The supersize **Super 8** (4250 Koval Lane, 702/794-0888, $45-100), just east of Bally's and Paris, is the chain's largest in the world. It offers a heated pool but no other resort amenities; on the other hand, it doesn't charge resort fees. There's free Internet access but not much of a budget for decor in the guest rooms or common areas. Stop at **Ellis Island Casino & Brewery** next door for ribs and microbrews.

Another group of motels clings to the south side of the convention center on Paradise and Desert Inn Roads as well as the west side between Paradise Road and the Strip on Convention Center Drive. If you're attending a convention and plan well in advance, you can reserve a very reasonable and livable room at any of several motels within a five-minute walk of the convention floor. Most of them have plenty of weekly rooms with kitchenettes, which can save you a bundle. It's a joy to be able to leave the convention floor and walk over to your room and back again if necessary—the shuttle buses to the far-flung hotels are very often crowded, slow, and inconvenient. Even if you're not attending a convention, this is a good part of town to stay in, off the main drag but in the middle of everything. You won't find whirlpool tubs, white-beach pools, or Egyptian cotton at **Rodeway Inn** (220 Convention Center Dr., 702/735-4151, $45-60), but you will find everything the budget traveler could ask for: hot showers, clean beds, and a refreshing pool. You'll also get extras such as a free continental breakfast and Wi-Fi. **Royal Resort** (99 Convention Center Dr., 702/735-6117 or 800/634-6118, $69-229) is part timeshare, part hotel. Its outdoor pool area nestles against tropical landscaping, private cabanas, and a new hot tub.

Downtown

Glitter Gulch fills Fremont Street from South Main Street to South 4th Street, but beyond that and on side streets, bargain-basement motels are numerous. Dozens of places are bunched together in three main groupings. It's not the best part of town, but it's certainly not the worst, and security is usually seen to by the management (but check with them to make sure). The motels along East Fremont Street and Las Vegas Boulevard North are the least expensive. Motels between downtown and the Strip on Las Vegas Boulevard South are slightly more expensive and in a slightly better neighborhood.

East Fremont Street has plenty of motels, sometimes one right next to another or separated by car dealerships and bars. It's a few minutes' drive to the downtown casinos and an excursion to the Strip. This is also RV country, with RV parks lining the highway past motel row and the big parking lots at the casinos. And with so many possibilities, it's a good stretch to cruise if you don't have reservations and most "No Vacancy" signs are lit.

Two reliable standards in this neighborhood, with guest rooms under $50, are Lucky Cuss (3305 Fremont St., 702/457-1929) and Downtowner (129 N. 8th St., 702/384-1441).

Las Vegas Boulevard North from Fremont Street to East Bonanza Road, along with North Main Street and the north-numbered streets from 6th to 13th, are also packed with motels one after the other. Stay on the lighted streets. It might be a little unnerving to deal with the front desk person through bars, but Glitter Gulch is very handy if that's where you want to spend your time, and these rooms can be amazingly reasonable if a room is not where you want to spend your money. The Bonanza Lodge (1808 Fremont St., 702/382-3990, from $50) offers the basics with double rooms with two beds. The Super 8 (700 Fremont St., 866/539-0036, from $69) is nicer, and the rates are higher.

The motels on Las Vegas Boulevard South between downtown and the north end of the Strip at Sahara Avenue have the most convenient location if you like to float between downtown and the Strip or if you're getting married in one of the wedding chapels that line this stretch of the boulevard. It's also brighter and busier, and right on the main bus routes. Most of these motels also offer weekly room rates with or without kitchenettes. The High Hat (1300 Las Vegas Blvd. S., 702/382-8080, $50-100 d) has been around for several years.

Hostels

It's hard to beat these places for budget accommodations. They offer rock-bottom prices for no-frills "rack rooms," singles, and doubles. Downtown choices include Hostel Cat (1236 Las Vegas Blvd. S., 702/380-6902, $18-40). Las Vegas Hostel (1322 Fremont St., 702/385-1150 or 800/550-8958, $24-45) has a swimming pool and a hot tub. The rates include a pancake breakfast, pool and foosball, and wireless Internet connections. The hostel also arranges trips to the Strip and visits to the Grand Canyon and other outdoorsy attractions.

Reserved only for international and student travelers (ID required), the dorms at Sin City Hostel (1208 Las Vegas Blvd. S., 702/868-0222, $18.50-22.50) fit the starving student's budget and include breakfast. Located on the Strip, the hostel features a barbecue pit, a basketball court, and Wi-Fi.

RV Parking
Casino RV Parking

A number of casinos have attached RV parks. Other casinos allow RVs to park overnight in their parking lots but have no facilities.

KOA at Circus Circus (2800 Las Vegas Blvd. S., 702/794-3757 or 800/562-7270, about $50) is a prime spot for RVers, especially those with kids, who want to be right in the thick of things but also want to take advantage of very good facilities. The big park is all paved, with a few grassy islands and shade trees; the convenience store is open daily 24 hours. Ten minutes spent learning where the Industrial Road back entrance is will save hours of sitting in traffic on the Strip. The park has 399 spaces operated by KOA. All have full hookups with 20-, 30-, and 50-amp power, and 280 of the spaces are pull-through. Tent sites (about $10) are also available. Wheelchair-accessible restrooms have flush toilets and hot showers, and there's also a laundry, a game room, a fenced playground, a heated swimming pool, a children's pool, a spa, a sauna, and groceries.

Sam's Town Nellis RV Park (4040 S. Nellis Blvd., 702/456-7777 or

800/634-6371, $18-25) has 500 spaces for motor homes, all with full hookups and 20-, 30-, and 50-amp power. It's mostly a paved parking lot with spacious sites, a heated pool, and a spa; the rec hall has a pool table and a kitchen. And, of course, it's near the bowling, dining, and movie theater in the casino.

Arizona Charlie's East (4445 Boulder Hwy., 800/970-7280, $32) has 239 spaces.

RV Parks

The best of the RV parks are more expensive than the casino RV parks, but the amenities—especially the atmosphere, views, and landscaping—are worth the price.

The **Hitchin' Post** (3640 Las Vegas Blvd. N., 702/644-1043 or 888/433-8402, $35-42) offers a pool, 24-hour saloon, a new dog wash, free cable TV, and Wi-Fi at its 196 spaces. The northern Las Vegas location is perhaps not the most desirable, but security is never a problem at the park. It's clean, and the on-site restaurant-bar rustles up a nice steak.

Oasis RV Park (2711 W. Windmill Lane, 800/566-4707, $46-80) is directly across I-15 from the Silverton Casino. Take Exit 33 for Blue Diamond Road, 3 miles south of Russell Road, then go east to Las Vegas Boulevard South. Turn right and drive one block to West Windmill, then turn right into the park. Opened in 1996, Oasis has 936 spaces, and huge date palms usher you from the park entrance to the cavernous 24,000-square-foot clubhouse. Each space is wide enough for a car and motor home and comes with a picnic table and patio. The foliage is plentiful and flanks an 18-hole putting course along with family and adult swimming pools. The resort features a full calendar of poker tournaments, movies, karaoke, and bar and restaurant specials. Wheelchair-accessible restrooms have flush toilets and hot showers; there is also a laundry, a grocery store, an exercise room, and an arcade.

Food

Las Vegas buffets have evolved from little better than fast food to lavish spreads of worldwide cuisine complete with fresh salads, comforting soups, and decadent desserts. The exclusive resorts on the Strip have developed their buffets into gourmet presentations, often including delicacies such as crab legs, crème brûlée, and even caviar. Others, especially the locals' casinos and those downtown that cater to more down-to-earth tastes, remain low-cost belly-filling options for intense gamblers and budget-conscious families. The typical buffet breakfast presents the usual fruits, juices, croissants, steam-table scrambled eggs, sausages, potatoes, and pastries. Lunch is salads and chicken, pizza, spaghetti, tacos, and more. Dinner is salads, steam-table vegetables, and potatoes with several varieties of meat, including a carving table with prime rib, turkey, and pork.

Buffets are still a big part of the Las Vegas vacation aura, but when the town's swank and swagger came back in the 1990s, it brought sophisticated dining with it. Las Vegas has come a long way from the coffee-and-sandwich shop shoved in a casino corner so players could recharge quickly and rush back to reclaim their slot machine.

Most major hotels have a 24-hour coffee shop, a steak house, and a buffet along with a couple of international restaurants. Noncasino restaurants around town are also proliferating quickly. Best of all, menu prices, like room rates, are consistently less expensive in Las Vegas than in any other major city in the country.

Upper Strip
Breakfast

It's all about hen fruit at ★ **The Egg and I** (4533 W. Sahara Ave., 702/364-9686, daily 6am-3pm, $10-20). They serve other breakfast fare as well, of course—the banana muffins and French toast are notable—but if you don't order an omelet, you're just being stubborn. It has huge portions, fair prices, and on-top-of-it service. Go!

The retro-deco gaudiness of the neon decor and bachelor pad-esque sunken fire pit may not do wonders for a Vegas-sized headache, but the tostada omelet at the **Peppermill Restaurant & Fireside Lounge** (2985 Las Vegas Blvd. S., 702/735-4177, daily 24 hours, $10-20) will give it what-for. For a little less zest, try the french toast ambrosia.

French and Continental

The pink accents at **Pamplemousse** (400 E. Sahara Ave., 702/733-2066, daily 5pm-10pm, $35-50) hint at the name's meaning (grapefruit) and set the stage for cuisine so fresh that the menu changes daily. If you eschew the prix fixe menu and order à la carte, ask about prices to avoid surprises. Specialties include leg and breast of duck in cranberry-raspberry sauce and a terrific escargot appetizer with butter, shallots, and red wine sauce.

Italian

Wall frescoes put you on an Italian thoroughfare as you dine on authentic cuisine at **Fellini's** (Stratosphere, 2000 Las Vegas Blvd. S., 702/383-4859, daily 5pm-11pm, $25-45). Each smallish dining room has a different fresco. The food is more the American idea of classic Italian than authentic, but only food snobs will find anything to complain about.

Steak

The perfectly cooked steaks and attentive service that once attracted Frank Sinatra, Nat "King" Cole, Natalie Wood, and Elvis are still trademarks at **Golden Steer** (308 W. Sahara Ave., 702/384-4470, daily 5pm-11pm, $35-50). A gold-rush motif and 1960s swankiness still abide here, along with classics like crab cakes, big hunks of beef, and Caesar salad prepared tableside.

Vegas Views

The 360-seat, 360-degree **Top of the World** (Stratosphere, 2000 Las Vegas Blvd. S., 702/380-7777 or 800/998-6937, daily 11am-11pm, $50-70), on the 106th floor of Stratosphere Tower more than 800 feet above the Strip, makes a complete revolution once every 80 minutes, giving you the full city panorama during dinner. The view of Vegas defies description, and the food is a recommendable complement. Order the seafood fettuccine or surf-and-turf gnocchi with lobster and beef short rib.

Center Strip
Asian

You may pay for the setting as much as for the food at **Fin** (The Mirage, 3400 Las Vegas Blvd. S., 866/339-4566, Thurs.-Mon. 5pm-10pm, $30-55). But why not? Sometimes the atmosphere is worth it, especially when you're trying to make an impression on your mate or potential significant other. The metallic-ball curtains evoke a rainstorm in a Chinese garden and set just the right romantic but noncloying mood. Still, we have to agree that while the prices are not outrageous, the food is not gourmet quality either; you can probably find more yum for your yuan elsewhere.

Better value can be had at **Tao** (Venetian, 3377 Las Vegas Blvd. S., 702/388-8338, Sun.-Fri. 5pm-midnight, Sat. 5pm-1am, $30-40), where pan-Asian dishes—the roasted Thai Buddha chicken is our pick—and an extensive sake selection are served in decor that is a trip through Asian history, from the Silk Road to Eastern spiritualism, including imperial koi ponds and feng shui aesthetics.

At **Wing Lei** (Wynn, 3131 Las Vegas Blvd. S., daily 5:30pm-10pm, $30-60), French colonialism comes through in chef Ming Yu's Shanghai style.

Breakfast

Any meal is a treat at **Tableau** (Wynn,

3131 Las Vegas Blvd. S., 702/248-DINE—702/248-3463 or 800/352-DINE—800/352-3463, daily 7am-2:30pm, $17-25), but the duck hash and eggs and the new summer squash and cherry tomato frittata in the garden atrium make breakfast the most important meal of the day at Wynn.

Buffets

The best buffet for under $85 in Las Vegas is, without a doubt, the **Village Seafood Buffet** (Rio, 3700 W. Flamingo Rd., 702/777-7943, daily 3:30pm-9:30pm, adults $45, age 4-10 $25). Vibrant maritime sculptures, watery blue-and-white decor, a cool sound system, and video screens put patrons in the mood, and garlic butter lobster tails are the main attraction. Other seafood preparations include grilled scallops, shrimp, mussels, and calamari with assorted vegetables and sauces, snow crab legs, oysters on the half shell, peel-and-eat shrimp, and steamed clams. There's even hand-carved prime rib, ham, chicken, and pasta for the nonfan of seafood. If you have room, the buffet serves 20 varieties of gelato.

Many people give the Rio top marks as the best "traditional" buffet near the center Strip, but we think it has been overtaken by **The Buffet at TI** (3300 Las Vegas Blvd. S., 702/894-7355, Mon.-Fri. 7am-10pm, breakfast $18, lunch $21, dinner $26, weekend brunch $24). The offerings are mostly standard—barbecue ribs, pizza, Chinese—but the ingredients are the freshest we've found on a buffet, and the few nontraditional buffet selections (especially the sushi and made-to-order pasta) make the higher-than-average price worthwhile.

French and Continental

The vanilla mousse-colored banquettes and chocolate swirl of the dark wood grain tables at **Payard Patisserie & Bistro** (Caesars Palace, 3570 Las Vegas Blvd. S., 702/731-7292 or 866/462-5982, daily 6:30am-2:30pm, $15-25,

pastry counter daily 6am-11pm) evoke the delightful French pastries for which François Payard is famous. Indeed, the bakery takes up most of the restaurant, tantalizing visitors with cakes, tarts, and petits fours. But the restaurant, open only for breakfast and lunch, stands on its own, with the quiches and paninis taking best in show.

Italian

It's no surprise that a casino named after the most romantic of Italian cities would be home to one of the best Italian restaurants around. **Canaletto** (Venetian, 3355 Las Vegas Blvd. S., 702/733-0070, Sun.-Thurs. 11am-11pm, Fri.-Sat. 11am-midnight, $15-25) focuses on Venetian cuisine. The kitchen staff performs around the grill and rotisserie—a demonstration kitchen—creating sumptuously authentic dishes. The spicy penne arrabiata gets our vote.

You can almost picture Old Blue Eyes himself between shows, twirling linguini and holding court at **Sinatra** (Encore, 3131 Las Vegas Blvd. S., 702/770-5320 or 888/352-DINE—888/352-3463, daily 5:30pm-10:30pm, $30-50). The Chairman's voice wafts through the speakers, and his photos and awards decorate the walls while you tuck into classic Italian food tinged with chef Theo Schoenegger's special touches.

Likewise, the "Old Vegas" vibe is thick at **Piero's** (355 Convention Center Dr., 702/369-2305, daily 5pm-10pm, $30-50). As enchanting as the exotic animal lithographs on the walls, Piero's has attracted celebrities ranging from Dick Van Dyke to Larry Bird. The decor, colorful owner Freddie Glusman, and low-key sophistication give the place a vaguely speakeasy feel.

Seafood

Submerse yourself in the cool, fluid, atmosphere at **AquaKnox** (Venetian, 3355 Las Vegas Blvd. S., 702/414-3772, Sun.-Thurs. noon-3pm and 5:30pm-11pm,

Fri.-Sat. noon-3pm and 5:30pm-11:30pm, $40-70). Its cobalt and cerulean tableware and design elements suggest a sea-sprayed embarcadero. The fish soup is the signature entrée, but the crab dishes are the way to go. If you can't bring yourself to order the crab-stuffed lobster, at least treat yourself to the crab cake appetizer.

Although it's named for the Brazilian beach paradise, Búzio's (Rio, 3700 W. Flamingo Rd., 702/777-7697, Wed.-Sun. 5pm-11pm, $30-45) serves its fish American and South American style. Hawaiian ahi, Maine lobster, Alaskan crab, and Chilean sea bass are always fresh and presented in perfect complement with tomato reductions, soy emulsions, and butter sauces.

Shrimp Cocktail

Don't let the presentation—lettuce leaf, scoop of bay shrimp, dollop of cocktail sauce, and a lemon wedge in a plastic cup—turn you off. The shrimp cocktail served at Haute Doggery (Linq, 3545 Las Vegas Blvd. S., Suite L-30, 702/430-4435, daily 10am-midnight, $1) is heaven.

Vegas Views

West Coast fixture Sushi Roku (Caesars Palace, 3570 Las Vegas Blvd. S., 702/733-7373, Sun.-Thurs. noon-10pm, Fri.-Sat. noon-11pm, $25-40) has terrific views both inside and out. Within the restaurant is a veritable Zen garden, bamboo, and shadowy table alcoves. Outside are unparalleled views up and down the Strip. Linq's High Roller across the street makes sharp contrast to the Japanese fantasy feel.

More Strip views await at Voodoo Steak (Rio, 3700 W. Flamingo Rd., 702/777-7800, daily 5pm-11pm, $30-60) along with steaks with a N'awlins creole and Cajun touch. Getting to the restaurant and the lounge requires a mini thrill ride to the top of the Rio tower in the glass elevator. The Rio contends that the restaurant is on the 51st floor and the lounge is on the 52nd floor, but they're really on the 41st and 42nd floors, respectively—Rio management dropped floors 40-49 as the number 4 has an ominous connotation in Chinese culture. Whatever floors they're on, the Voodoo double-decker provides a great view of the Strip. The food and drink are expensive and tame, but the fun is in the overlook, especially if you eat or drink outside on the decks.

Lower Strip
Asian

Voted one of Zagat's favorite restaurants in Vegas, China Grill (Mandalay Bay, 3950 Las Vegas Blvd. S., 702/632-7404, Sun.-Thurs. 5pm-11pm, Fri.-Sat. 5pm-midnight, $30-45) is another one of Mandalay Bay's architecturally arresting designer restaurants, using a crystal foot bridge, multiple levels, a light-projected ceiling, and the ubiquitous exhibition kitchen to heighten the dining experience. Signature specialties include exotic twists on traditional Chinese favorites (we suggest the grilled garlic shrimp or lobster pancakes with red curry coconut sauce). More traditional, expensive, and classic is China Grill's next-door neighbor, Shanghai Lilly (3950 Las Vegas Blvd. S., 702/632-7409, Mon. 5:30pm-10:30pm, Thurs.-Sun. 5:30pm-11pm, $32-52), where Cantonese and Szechuan creations reign supreme and the decor is understated and elegant.

Chinese art in a Hong Kong bistro setting with fountain and lake views make Jasmine (Bellagio, 3600 Las Vegas Blvd. S., daily 5:30pm-10:30pm, $40-60) one of the most visually striking Chinese restaurants in town. The food is classic European-influenced Cantonese.

Breakfast

The Veranda (Four Seasons, 3960 Las Vegas Blvd. S., 702/632-5000, daily 6:30am-10pm, $25-40) transforms itself from a light, airy, indoor-outdoor breakfast and lunch nook into a late dinner spot oozing with South Seas ambiance and a check total worthy of a Four Seasons restaurant. As you might expect from the name, dining on the terrace is a favorite among well-to-do locals, especially for brunch on spring and fall weekends.

Buffets

If you think "Las Vegas buffet" means a call to the trough of mediocre cheap prices and get-what-you-pay-for food quality, Bally's would like to invite you and your credit card to the **Sterling Brunch** (702/967-7999, Sun. 9:30am-2:30pm, $85). That's right, $85 for one meal, per person, and you have to fetch your own vittles. But the verdict is almost unanimous: It's worth it, especially if you load up on the grilled lobster, filet mignon, caviar, sushi, Mumm champagne, and other high-dollar offerings. Leave the omelets and salads for IHOP; a plateful of sinful tarts and chocolate indulgence is a must, along with just one more glass of champagne.

On the other hand, for the price of that one brunch at Bally's, you can eat for three days at the **Roundtable Buffet** (Excalibur, 3580 Las Vegas Blvd. S., daily 7am-10pm, breakfast $15, lunch $16, dinner $20, ages 4-12 get $4 off). The Excalibur started the trend of the all-day-long buffet, and the hotel sells all-day wristbands for $30. If that's not enough gluttony for you, the wristband also serves as a line pass. The **French Market Buffet** (The Orleans, 4500 W. Tropicana Ave., 702/365-7111, Mon.-Sat. 8am-4pm, Sun. 8am-9pm, breakfast $8, lunch $9, dinner $14-19, Sun. brunch $15, ages 4-7 get $3 off) has a similar all-day deal for $24 (Fri. $27).

French and Continental

The steaks and seafood at ★ **Mon Ami Gabi** (Paris, 3655 Las Vegas Blvd. S., 702/944-4224, Sun.-Fri. 7am-11pm, Sat. 7am-midnight, $20-35) are comparable to those at any fine Strip establishment—at about half the price. It's a bistro, so you

know the crepes and other lunch specials are terrific, but you're better off coming for dinner. Try the trout Grenobloise.

Award-winning chef Andre Rochat lays claim to two top French establishments on this end of the Strip. **Andre's** (Monte Carlo, 3770 Las Vegas Blvd. S., 702/798-7151, Tues.-Sun. 5:30pm-10pm, $35-55) has an up-to-date yet old-country feel, with smoky glass, silver furnishings, and teal-and-cream accents. The menu combines favorites from around the world with French sensibilities to create unique "French fusion" fare, such as lamb with curried risotto and goat cheese or a peppercorn and cognac cream sauce for the delectable fillet of beef. The cellar is befitting one of the best French restaurants in town, and the selection of port, cognac, and other after-dinner drinks is unparalleled. Rochat's **Alizé** (Palms, 4321 W. Flamingo Rd., 702/951-7000, daily 5:30pm-10pm, $40-60) is similar but includes a sweet Strip view from atop the Palms.

When you name your restaurant after a maestro, you're setting some pretty high standards for your food. Fortunately, **Picasso** (Bellagio, 3600 Las Vegas Blvd. S., 702/693-7223, Wed.-Mon. 6pm-9:30pm, $113-123) is up to the self-inflicted challenge. With limited seating in its Picasso-canvassed dining room and a small dining time window, the restaurant has a couple of prix fixe menus. It's seriously expensive, and if you include Kobe beef, lobster, wine pairings, and a cheese course, you and a mate could easily leave several pounds heavier and $500 lighter.

Gastropub

Inside the Hard Rock Casino, ★ **Culinary Dropout** (4455 Paradise Rd., 702/522-8100, www.culinarydropout.com, Mon.-Thurs. 11am-11pm, Fri. 11am-midnight, Sat. 10am-midnight, Sun. 10am-11pm, $10-27) takes comfort food seriously, with home-style favorites like fried chicken and grilled cheese sliders. The provolone fondue appetizer, accompanied by pillowy pretzel rolls, is a meal in itself.

Pizza

With lines snaking out its unmarked entrance, in a dark alleyway decorated with record covers, Secret Pizza (Cosmopolitan, 3708 Las Vegas Blvd. S., 3rd Fl., Fri.-Mon. 11am-5am, Tues.-Thurs. 11am-4am, slices $3-4) is not so secret anymore. Located next to Blue Ribbon Sushi on The Cosmopolitan's third floor, it's a great place to get a quick, greasy slice.

Seafood

Rick Moonen is the "it" chef of the moment, making his ★ RM Seafood (Mandalay Bay, 3950 Las Vegas Blvd. S., 702/632-9300, daily 11am-11pm, $35-55) the place to be seen whether you're a seafood junkie or just another pretty face. You can almost hear the tide-rigging whirr and the mahogany creak in the yacht-club restaurant setting. RM Upstairs delivers a tasty and reasonably priced tasting menu ($75) that recently featured beef tartare, foie gras, and baked salmon. You have to try the rabbit trio; it's available à la carte or on the tasting menu for a supplemental charge.

Steak

Bringing the lounge vibe to the restaurant setting is ★ N9NE (Palms, 4321 W. Flamingo Rd., 702/933-9900, Sun.-Thurs. 5:30pm-10pm, Fri.-Sat. 5:30pm-11pm, $55-85). Sleek furnishings of chrome highlighted by rich colored lighting add accompaniment, but N9NE never loses focus on its raison d'être: flawlessly prepared steak and seafood and impeccable service.

The care used by the small farms from which Tom Colicchio's Craftsteak (MGM Grand, 3799 Las Vegas Blvd. S., 702/891-7318, Tues.-Thurs. 5:30pm-10pm, Fri.-Mon. 6pm-10pm, $40-60) buys its ingredients is evident in the full flavor of the excellently seasoned steaks and chops. Spacious and bright with red lacquer and light woodwork, Craftsteak's decor is conducive to good times with friends and family and isn't overbearing or intimidating.

The original Gallagher's Steakhouse (New York New York, 3790 Las Vegas Blvd. S., 702/740-6450, Sun.-Thurs. 4pm-11pm, Fri.-Sat. 4pm-midnight, $30-42) has been an institution in New York City since 1927. The restaurant is decorated with memorabilia from the golden age of movies and sports. You'll know why the longevity is deserved after sampling its famed dry-aged beef and notable seafood selection.

Tapas

The Cosmopolitan's reinvention of the social club takes diners' taste buds to flavor nirvana. Equal parts supper club, nightclub, and jazz club, ★ Rose. Rabbit. Lie. (Cosmopolitan, 3708 Las Vegas Blvd. S., 702/698-7000, Tues.-Sat. 5:30pm-2am, $80-150) serves a mostly tapas-style menu. Sharing is encouraged, with about four small plates per person satisfying most appetites, especially if you splurge on the chocolate terrarium for dessert. The club is sectioned into several dining rooms with unique themes—pool room, music room, library—and cocktails. Expect varied entertainment throughout the evening (singers, dancers, magicians), but no one will blame you for focusing on the food and cocktails.

Vegas Views

Paris's Eiffel Tower Restaurant (3655 Las Vegas Blvd. S., 702/948-6937, Sun.-Thurs. 11:30am-2:30pm and 5pm-10pm, Fri.-Sat. 11:30am-2:30pm and 5pm-10:45pm, $35-55) hovers 100 feet above the Strip. Your first "show" greets you when the glass elevator opens onto the organized chaos of chef Jean Joho's kitchen. Order the soufflé, have a glass of wine, and bask in the romantic piano strains as the bilingual culinary staff performs delicate French culinary feats.

Downtown
Asian

A perfect little eatery for the budding Bohemia of East Fremont Street, ★ **Le Thai's** (523 E. Fremont St., 702/778-0888, Mon.-Thurs. 11am-11pm, Fri.-Sat. 11am-2am, $50-75) attracts a diverse clientele ranging from ex-yuppies to body-art lovers. Most come for the three-color curry, and you should too. There's nothing especially daring on the menu, but the *pad prik, ga pow,* and garlic fried rice are better than what's found at many Strip restaurants that charge twice as much. Choose your spice level wisely; Le Thai does not mess around.

Buffets

Assuming you're not a food snob, the **Garden Court Buffet** (Main Street Station, 200 N. Main St., 702/387-1896 or 800/713-8933, daily 7am-3pm and 4pm-10pm, breakfast $7, lunch $8, dinner $11-14, Fri. seafood $22) will satisfy your taste buds and your bank account. The fare is mostly standard, with some specialties designed to appeal to the casino's Asian and Pacific Islander target market. At **The Buffet** (Golden Nugget, 129 E. Fremont St., 702/385-7111, Mon.-Fri. 7am-10pm, Sat.-Sun. 7am-3:30pm, breakfast $12, lunch $14, dinner $20, weekend brunch $17, Fri.-Sun. seafood $24), the food leaves nothing to be desired, with extras like an omelet station, calzone, Greek salad, and a delicate fine banana cake putting it a cut above the ordinary buffet, especially for downtown. Glass and brass accents make for peaceful digestion.

French and Continental

Hugo's Cellar (Four Queens, 202 E. Fremont St., 702/385-4011, daily 5:30pm-10:30pm, $15-25) is romance from the moment each woman in your party receives her red rose until the last complimentary chocolate-covered strawberry is devoured. Probably the best gourmet room for the money, dimly lit Hugo's is located below the casino floor, shutting it off from the hubbub above. It is pricy, but the inclusion of sides, a mini dessert, and salad—prepared tableside with your choice of ingredients—helps ease the sticker shock. Sorbet is served between courses. The house appetizer is the Hot Rock, four meats sizzling on a lava slab; mix and match the meats with the dipping sauces.

Italian

Decidedly uncave-like with bright lights and an earthen-tile floor, **The Grotto** (Golden Nugget, 2300 S. Casino Dr., 702/386-8341, Sun.-Thurs. 11:30am-10:30pm, Fri.-Sat. 11:30am-11:30pm, $15-30) offers top-quality northern Italian fare with a view of the Golden Nugget's shark tank (ask for a window table). Portions are large, and the margaritas refreshing.

Seafood

The prime rib gets raves, but the seafood and the prices are the draw at **Second Street Grill** (Fremont, 200 Fremont St., 702/385-3232, Thurs. and Sun.-Mon. 5pm-10pm, Fri.-Sat. 5pm-11pm, $15-25). The grill bills itself as "American contemporary with Pacific Rim influence," and the menu reflects this Eastern inspiration with steaks and chops—but do yourself a favor and order the crab legs with lemon ginger butter.

Steaks and seafood get equal billing on the menu at **Triple George** (201 N. 3rd St., 702/384-2761, Mon.-Fri. 11am-10pm, Sat.-Sun. 4pm-10pm, $15-35), but again, the charbroiled salmon and the martinis are what brings the suave crowd back for more.

Shrimp Cocktail

The Golden Gate's **Du-Par's** (1 Fremont St., 702/385-1906, daily 11am-3am, $4) began serving a San Francisco-style shrimp cocktail in 1955, and more than 30 million have been served since. In fact, it's the oldest meal deal in Las Vegas—appropriate for the oldest hotel in Las Vegas. It goes great with a draft beer. Du-Par's Restaurant is also famous locally for melt-in-your-mouth pancakes.

Off the Strip

There are plenty of fine restaurants outside the resort corridor.

The congenial proprietor of ★ **Phat Phrank's** (4850 W. Sunset Rd., Mon.-Fri. 7am-7pm, Sat. 10am-3pm, $10-15) keeps the atmosphere light and the fish tacos crispy and delicious. Try all three of the house salsas; they're all great complements to all the offerings, especially the flavorful pork burrito and *adobada torta.*

Not only beatniks (or whatever the young whippersnappers are calling themselves these days) will dig the breakfast vibe at **The Beat** (520 E. Fremont St., 702/686-3164, Mon.-Thurs. 7am-7pm, Fri. 7am-10pm, Sat. 9am-10pm, $5-10) in the downtown arts district. The joe is from Colorado River Coffee Roasters in Boulder City, and the bread is from Bon Breads Baking in Las Vegas.

Thai Spice (4433 W. Flamingo Rd., 702/362-5308, Mon.-Thurs. 11:30am-10pm, Fri.-Sat. 11:30am-10:30pm, $10-17) gives Le Thai a run for its baht as best Thai restaurant in town; the soups, noodle dishes, traditional curries, pad thai, and egg rolls are all well prepared. Tell your waiter how hot you want your food on a scale of 1 to 10. The big numbers peg the needle on the Scoville scale, so beware.

Its delicious dim sum is no secret, so parking and seating are at a premium during lunch at **Cathay House** (5300 W. Spring Mountain Ave., 702/876-3838, daily 10:30am-10pm, $10-20) in Chinatown. Dim sum is available any time, but be a purist and only order it for lunch. For dinner, opt for orange beef or garlic chicken.

Shopping

Malls

The most upscale and most Strip-accessible of the traditional, non-casino-affiliated, indoor shopping complexes, **Fashion Show** (3200 Las Vegas Blvd. S., 702/784-7000, Mon.-Sat. 10am-9pm, Sun. 11am-7pm), across from the Wynn, is anchored by Saks Fifth Avenue, Dillard's, Neiman Marcus, Macy's, and Nordstrom. The mall gets its name from the 80-foot retractable runway in the Great Hall, where resident retailers put on fashion shows on weekend afternoons. Must-shop stores include Papyrus, specializing in stationery, greeting cards, calendars, and gifts centering on paper arts and crafts, and The LEGO Store, where blockheads can find specialty building sets tied to it movies, video games, and television shows, along with free monthly mini model-building workshops for kids and teens. The one-restaurant food court has something for every taste. Better yet, dine alfresco at a Strip-side café, shaded by "the cloud," a 128-foot-tall canopy that doubles as a projection screen.

If your wallet houses dozens of Ben Franklins, **Crystals at City Center** (3720 Las Vegas Blvd. S., 702/590-9299, Sun.-Thurs. 10am-11pm, Fri.-Sat. 10am-midnight) is your destination for impulse buys like a hand-woven Olimpia handbag from Bottega Veneta for her or a titanium timepiece from Porsche Design for him.

Parents can reward their children's patience with rides on cartoon animals, spaceships, and other kiddie favorites at two separate play areas in the **Meadows Mall** (4300 Meadows Lane, 702/878-3331, Mon.-Thurs. 10am-9pm, Fri.-Sun. 10am-10pm). There are more than 125 stores and restaurants—all the usual mall denizens along with some interesting specialty shops. It's across the street from the Las Vegas Springs Preserve, so families can make a day of it. The **Boulevard Mall** (3528 S. Maryland Pkwy., 702/735-8268,

Mon.-Sat. 10am-9pm, Sun. noon-7pm) is similar. It's in an older and less trendy setting, but a new facade, family attractions, and better dining are driving a comeback.

A visit to **Town Square** (6605 Town Center Dr., Las Vegas Blvd. S., 702/269-5000, Mon.-Thurs. 10am-9:30pm, Fri.-Sat. 10am-10pm, Sun. 11am-8pm) is like a stroll through a favorite suburb. "Streets" wind between stores in Spanish, Moorish, and Mediterranean-style buildings. Mall stalwarts like Victoria's Secret and Abercrombie & Fitch are here along with some unusual treats—Tommy Bahama's includes a café. Just like a real town, the retail outlets surround a central park, 13,000 square feet of mazes, tree houses, and performance stages. Around holiday time, machine-made snowflakes drift down through the trees. Nightlife, from laid-back wine and martini bars to rousing live entertainment as well as the 18-screen Rave movie theater, round out a trip into "town."

Easterners and Westerners alike revel in the wares offered at **Chinatown Plaza** (4255 Spring Mountain Rd., 702/221-8448, Mon.-Fri. 9am-10pm, Sat.-Sun. 10am-11pm). Despite the pan-Asian name, Chinatown Las Vegas is a pan-Asian clearinghouse where Asians can celebrate their history and heritage while stocking up on favorite reminders of home. Meanwhile, Westerners can submerge themselves in new cultures by sampling the offerings at authentic Chinese, Thai, Vietnamese, and other Asian restaurants and strolling the plaza reading posters explaining Chinese customs. Tea sets, silk robes, Buddha statuettes, and jade carvings are of particular interest, as is the Diamond Bakery with its elaborate wedding cakes and sublime mango mousse cake.

Casino Plazas

Caesars Palace initiated the concept of Las Vegas as a shopping destination in 1992 when it unveiled the **Forum Shops** (702/893-4800 or 800/CAESARS—800/223-7277, Sun.-Thurs.

10am-11pm, Fri.-Sat. 10am-midnight). Top brand luxury stores coexist with fashionable hipster boutiques amid some of the best people-watching on the Strip. A stained glass-domed pedestrian plaza greets shoppers as they enter the 175,000-square-foot expansion from the Strip. You'll find one of only two spiral escalators in the United States. When you're ready for a break, the gods come alive hourly to extract vengeance in the *Fall of Atlantis* and *Festival Fountain Show*; or check out the feeding of the fish in the big saltwater aquarium twice daily.

Part shopping center, part theater in the round, the **Miracle Mile** (Planet Hollywood, 3663 Las Vegas Blvd. S., 702/866-0703 or 888/800-8284, Sun.-Thurs. 10am-11pm, Fri.-Sat. 10am-midnight) is a delightful (or vicious, depending on your point of view) circle of shops, eateries, bars, and theaters. If your budget doesn't quite stand up to the Forum Shops, Miracle Mile could be just your speed. Low-cost shows include tributes to Elvis and the Beatles, the campy *Evil Dead—The Musical* and *Zombie Burlesque,* and family-friendly animal acts and magicians.

Las Vegas icon Rita Rudner loves the **Grand Canal Shoppes** (Venetian, 3377 Las Vegas Blvd. S., 702/414-4500, Sun.-Thurs. 10am-11pm, Fri.-Sat. 10am-midnight) because "Where else but in Vegas can you take a gondola to the Gap?" And where else can you be serenaded by opera singers while trying on shoes? (It's worth noting there's not really a Gap here—The Venetian is way too upscale for such a pedestrian store.) The shops line the canal among streetlamps and cobblestones under a frescoed sky. Nature gets a digital assist in the photos for sale at Peter Lik gallery, and Michael Kors and Diane von Furstenberg compete for your shopping dollar. The "Streetmosphere" includes strolling minstrels and specialty acts, and many of these entertainers find their way to St. Mark's Square for seemingly impromptu performances.

Money attracts money, and Steve Wynn was able lure Oscar de la Renta and Jean Paul Gaultier to open their first retail stores in the country at the indulgent **Esplanade** (Wynn, 3131 Las Vegas Blvd. S., 702/770-7000, daily 10am-11pm). A cursory look at the tenant stores is enough to convince you that the Esplanade caters to the wealthy, the lucky, and the reckless: Hermès, Manolo Blahnik, and even Ferrari are at home under stained-glass skylights.

Perfectly situated in the flourishing urban arts district, the **Downtown Container Park** (707 E. Fremont St., 702/637-4244, Mon.-Thurs. 11am-9pm, Fri.-Sat. 11am-10pm, Sun. 11am-8pm) packs 50 boutiques, galleries, bars, and bistros into their own shipping containers. The business names hint at the hip, playful atmosphere: Crazylegs (women's clothes), The Rusty Nail (housewares), Lead in the Window (stained glass).

Unless you're looking for a specific item or brand, or you're attracted to the atmosphere, attractions, architecture, or vibe of a particular Strip destination, you can't go wrong browsing the one in your hotel. You'll find other shops just as nice at **Le Boulevard** (Paris, 3655 Las Vegas Blvd. S., 702/739-4111, daily 8am-2am), **Grand Bazaar Shops** (Bally's, 3645 Las Vegas Blvd. S., 702/967-4366 or 888/266-5687, daily 10am-11pm), **Linq** (3545 Las Vegas Blvd. S., 702/694-8100 or 866/328-1888, shop and restaurant hours vary), and **Mandalay Place** (Mandalay Bay, 3930 Las Vegas Blvd. S., 702/632-7777 or 877/632-7800, daily 10am-11pm).

Information and Services

Information Bureaus

The **Las Vegas Convention and Visitors Authority** (LVCVA, 3150 Paradise Rd., 702/892-0711 or 877/VISIT-LV—877/847-4858, www.lvcva.

com, daily 8am-5pm) maintains a website of special hotel deals and other offers at www.lasvegas.com. One of LVCVA's priorities is filling hotel rooms—call its reservations service at 877/VISIT-LV—877/847-4858. You can also call the same number for convention schedules and entertainment offerings.

The **Las Vegas Chamber of Commerce** (6671 Las Vegas Blvd. S., 702/735-1616, www.lvchamber.com) has a bunch of travel resources and fact sheets on its website. **Vegas.com** is a good resource for up-to-the-minute show schedules and reviews.

Visitors Guides and Magazines

Nearly a dozen free periodicals for visitors are available in various places around town—racks in motel lobbies and by the bell desks of the large hotels are the best bet. They all cover basically the same territory—showrooms, lounges, dining, dancing, buffets, gambling, sports, events, coming attractions—and most have numerous ads that will transport coupon clippers to discount heaven.

Anthony Curtis's monthly *Las Vegas Advisor* (www.lasvegasadvisor.com) ferrets out the best dining, entertainment, gambling, and hotel room values, shows, and restaurants, and presents them objectively (no advertising or comps accepted). A year's subscription is only $50 ($37 for an electronic subscription) and includes exclusive coupons worth more than $3,000. Sign up online.

Today in Las Vegas (www.todayinlv.com) is a 64-page weekly mini magazine bursting its staples with listings, coupons, previews, maps, and restaurant overviews. To get an issue ($4.95) before you leave on your trip, visit the website.

The digital magazine *What's On* (www.whats-on.com) provides comprehensive information along with entertainer profiles, articles, calendars, phone numbers, and lots of ads. The online edition and the newsletter are free but require registration.

◈ Side Trip to Hoover Dam

The 1,400-mile Colorado River has been carving and gouging great canyons and valleys with red sediment-laden waters for 10 million years. For 10,000 years Native Americans, the Spanish, and Mormon settlers coexisted with the fitful river, rebuilding after spring floods and withstanding the droughts that often reduced the mighty waterway to a muddy trickle in fall. But the 1905 flood convinced the Bureau of Reclamation to "reclaim" the West, primarily by building dams and canals. The most ambitious of these was Hoover Dam: 40 million cubic yards of reinforced concrete, turbines, and transmission lines.

Hoover Dam remains an engineering marvel, attracting millions of visitors each year. It makes an interesting half-day escape from the glitter of Las Vegas, only 30 miles to the north. The one-hour Dam Tour (every 30 minutes, daily 9:30am-3:30pm, ages 8 and over, $30) offers a guided exploration of its power plant and walkways, along with admission to the visitors center. The two-hour Power Plant Tour (adults $15, seniors, children, and military $12, uniformed military and under age 4 free) focuses on the dam's construction and engineering through multimedia presentations, exhibits, docent talk, and a power plant tour.

Getting There

The bypass bridge diverts traffic away from Hoover Dam, saving time and headaches for both drivers and dam visitors. Still, the 35-mile drive from central Las Vegas to a parking lot at the dam will take 45 minutes or more. From the Strip, I-15 South connects with I-215 southeast of the airport, and I-215 East takes drivers to US-93 in Henderson. Remember that US-93 shares the roadway with US-95 and I-515 till well past Henderson. Going south on US-93, exit at NV-172 to the dam. Note that this route is closed on the Arizona side; drivers continuing on to the Grand Canyon must retrace NV-172 to US-93 and cross the bypass bridge. A parking garage ($10) is convenient to the visitors center and dam tours, but free parking is available at turnouts on both sides of the dam for those willing to walk.

The 150-page *Showbiz Weekly* (http://lasvegasmagazine.com) spotlights performers and has listings and ads for shows, lounges, and buffets. Subscribe or buy single digital issue online.

The annual publication *Las Vegas Perspective* (www.lvperspective.com) is chock-full of area demographics as well as retail, real estate, and community statistics, updated every year.

Services

If you need the police, the fire department, or an ambulance in an emergency, dial 911.

The centrally located University Medical Center (1800 W. Charleston Blvd., at Shadow Lane, 702/383-2000) has 24-hour emergency service, with outpatient and trauma-care facilities. Hospital emergency rooms throughout the valley are open 24 hours, as are many privately run quick-care centers.

Most hotels will have lists of dentists and doctors, and the Clark County Medical Society (2590 E. Russell Rd., 702/739-9989, www.clarkcountymedical.org) website lists members based on specialty. You can also get a physician referral from Desert Springs Hospital (702/733-6875 or 800/842-5439).

Getting Around

Car

Downtown Las Vegas crowds around the junction of I-15, US-95, and US-93. I-15 runs from Los Angeles (272 miles, 4-5 hours' drive) to Salt Lake City (419 miles, 6-8 hours). US-95 meanders from Yuma, Arizona, on the Mexican border, up the western side of Nevada, through Coeur D'Alene, Idaho, all the way up to British Columbia, Canada. US-93 starts in Phoenix and hits Las Vegas 285 miles later, then merges with I-15 for a while only to fork off and shoot straight up the east side of Nevada and continue due north all the way to Alberta, Canada.

Car Rental

When you call around to rent, ask what the *total* price of your car is going to be. With sales tax, use tax, airport fees, and other miscellaneous charges, you can pay as much as 20 percent over and above the quoted rate. Typical shoulder-season weekly rates run from about $140 for economy and compact cars to $250 for vans and $400 for luxury sedans, but prices increase by one-third or more during major conventions and holiday periods. One recent holiday week saw economy car rates at about $230 across the board. Parking is free in casino surface lots and garages. Check with your insurance agent at home about coverage on rental cars; often your insurance covers rental cars (minus your deductible), and you won't need the rental company's. If you rent a car on most credit cards, you get automatic rental-car insurance coverage. Las Vegas rental car rates change as fast as hotel room rates, depending on the season, day of the week, and convention traffic.

Most of the large car-rental companies have desks at the McCarran Rent-A-Car Center (702/261-6001). Dedicated McCarran shuttles leave the main terminal from outside exit doors 10 and 11 about every five minutes bound for the Rent-A-Car Center. Taxicabs are also available at the center. Companies represented at the center include Advantage (800/777-9377), Alamo (800/GO-ALAMO—800/462-5266), Avis (800/331-1212), Budget (800/922-2899), and Dollar (800/800-4000). The others—Enterprise (800/RENTACAR—800/736-8222), Hertz (800/654-3131), Payless (800/729-5377), Sav-Mor (800/634-6779), and Thrifty (800/367-2277) pick up customers at the center. When arriving at Terminal 1 or Terminal 3, follow the "Ground Transportation" signs to the Rental Car Shuttle staging area. A blue-and-white bus will pick you up in less than five minutes for the three-mile trip to the Rent-A-Car Center. Of course, the buses will ferry you from the rental drop-off area back to the airport when your trip is over.

RV Rental

Travelers using Las Vegas as their base or departure point can rent virtually any type of recreational vehicle, from pickup truck-mounted coaches to 40-foot Class A rolling mansions. El Monte RV (13001 Las Vegas Blvd. S., Henderson, 702/269-8000 or 866/337-2214) south of town (take I-15 South, exiting at St. Rose Parkway; head east to Las Vegas Boulevard and drive south) and on the east side (3800 Boulder Hwy., 702/269-8000 or 866/337-2214) deals primarily in Class C "cab-over" models and Class A rock-star tour bus behemoths. Base prices for the Class C cab-overs start at about $600-800 per week, but miles—bundled in 100-mile packages—and incidentals such as kitchenware, pillows, coffeemakers, and toasters can easily increase the total by 75 percent. El Monte's big dog, an EMW AC37 Slideout, goes for $1,750 per week before mileage and extras.

Cruise America (551 N. Gibson Rd., Henderson, 888/980-8282) on the southeast side (take US-95 south to the Sunset Road exit east; turn right on Gibson Road) touts its exclusively cab-over fleet as having more ready-to-use sleep space and maneuverability. Its RVs range 19-30 feet, suitable for parties of 3-7 people. Seven-night rentals average $430 to 900. The company adds a mileage estimate (at about 35 cents per mile) at the time of rental and adjusts the charges based on actual miles driven when you return the vehicle. Common extra charges include linens, kitchen equipment, and generator use.

Renting from the Camping World (13175 Las Vegas Blvd. S., 877/594-3353) store gives the added convenience of stocking up for your trip as you pick up your RV. Located virtually across the road from El Monte RV, Camping World's 24- to 28-foot "standard" rental, at $850 to $1,050 per week, sleeps six if you're all very friendly. A 32-foot Class A goes for $1,330 per week. Prices include insurance, but mileage and kitchen and linen kits are extra.

Monorail

Since 2004, the site of the new SLS Casino on the north end of the Strip and the MGM Grand near the south end have been connected via the Las Vegas Monorail (702/699-8200, Mon. 7am-midnight, Tues.-Thurs. 7am-2am, Fri.-Sun. 7am-3am, $5, 24-hour pass $12), with stops at the SLS, Westgate, Convention Center, Harrah's/Linq, Flamingo/Caesars Palace, Bally's/Paris, and MGM Grand. More than 30 major resorts are now within easy reach along the Strip without a car or taxi. Reaching speeds up to 50 mph, the monorail glides above traffic to cover the four-mile route in about 14 minutes. Nine trains with four air-conditioned cars each carry up to 152 riders along the elevated track running on the east side of the strip, stopping every few minutes at the stations. Tickets are available at vending machines at each station as well as at station properties.

Bus

Citizen Area Transit (CAT, 702/228-RIDE—702/228-7433, www.rtcsouthernnevada.com), the public bus system, is managed by the Regional Transportation Commission. CAT runs 54 routes all over Las Vegas Valley. Fares are $6 for two hours, $8 for 24 hours, free under age 5. Call or access the ride guide online. Bus service is pretty comprehensive, but even the express routes with fewer stops take a long time to get anywhere.

Taxi

Except for peak periods, taxis are numerous and quite readily available, and drivers are good sources of scuttlebutt (not always accurate) and entertainment (not always wholesome). Of course, Las Vegas operates at peak loads most of the time, so if you're not in a taxi zone right in front of one of the busiest hotels, it might be tough to get one. The 16 companies plying the streets of Las Vegas charge $3.30 for the flag drop and $2.60 per mile. Waiting time is $0.50 per minute.

Limo

Offering chauffeur-driven domestic and imported sedans, shuttle buses, and SUVs in addition to stretch and superstretch limos, Las Vegas Limousines (702/888-4848) can transport up to 20 people per vehicle to and from sporting events, corporate meetings, airport connections, bachelor and bachelorette parties, sightseeing tours, and more. Rates are $55 per hour for a six-seat stretch limo, $75 for a 10-seat superstretch.

Presidential Limousine (702/720-3225) charges $64 per hour for its stretch six-seater, $80 per hour for the superstretch eight-seater; both include TVs and video players, mobile phones, sparkling cider, and roses for the women. They don't include a mandatory fuel surcharge or driver gratuity.

Tours

Several companies offer the chance to see the sights of Las Vegas by bus, helicopter, airplane, or off-road vehicle. The ubiquitous Gray Line (702/739-7777 or 877/333-6556) offers tours of the city by night as well as tours of Hoover Dam and the Grand Canyon. City tours (Thurs.-Sat. 7pm, $59) visit the major Vegas free sights: the Bellagio Fountains and Conservatory, the "Welcome to Las Vegas" sign, the

◈ Southwest Side Trip

Las Vegas is located just outside the "Grand Circle"—the largest concentration of national parks and monuments in the country—making it a great base for visiting colorful canyons, inspiring geological formations, and living history. The Grand Canyon should be first the Southwestern park on your list, but nine other national parks are within 500 miles of Glitter Gulch.

Zion National Park is the most accessible (160 miles from Las Vegas), a straight shot up I-15 North for 128 miles to UT-9 for the final 32-mile stretch to the park. Zion's imposing monoliths, such as the Court of the Patriarchs, whose sandstone behemoths are named for Abraham, Isaac, and Jacob, contrast with the three serene Emerald Pools that reflect the region's features.

Continue on to Bryce Canyon (260 miles from Las Vegas; 72 miles from Zion) where it's easy to see why ancient Paiute people believed the narrow hoodoos were people turned to stone by angry gods. The haunting formations are the result of eons of the winds' and waters' masonry skills. From Zion, continue northeast on UT-9 for 13 miles to US-89 North for 43 miles to UT-12 East. Continue 14 miles to UT-63 South for two miles to the park gate.

Northeast of Bryce, Capitol Reef National Park (roughly 352 miles from Las Vegas; 112 miles from Bryce Canyon) is a vast network of natural bridges, domes and cliffs created by Waterpocket Fold, which was formed during an ancient geologic upheaval. From Bryce Canyon, take UT-63/Johns Valley Road/UT-22 North for 45 miles to UT-62 North for another 26 miles. Turn right onto Browns Lane for three miles. Then turn right onto UT-24 East/East 300 Street South for the final 38 miles.

Farther afield from Las Vegas are Arches National Park (453 miles) and Canyonlands National Park

(465 miles). The backdrop for any self-respecting western, Arches is home to Delicate Arch, as well as more than 2,000 other natural arches, fins, towers, and crevasses. I-15 will get you most of the way to either of these eastern Utah parks. To get to Arches, take I-15 North 426 miles to US-191, and follow it for 27 miles to Arches Entrance Road. Canyonlands was formed by the Colorado River system, which carved out its unique buttes, mesas, and sandstone spires. It's only 26 miles from Arches: Take US-191 North for 7 miles to UT-313; continue for 15 miles to Grand View point Road/Island in the Sky Road for four miles. To get to these two parks from Las Vegas, take I-15 for 243 miles to I-70 toward Denver. Follow I-70 for 182 miles, then take US-191 for 21 miles. A right turn onto UT-313 W will take you the last 19 miles to the parks.

Nevada's only national Park, Great Basin (296 miles from Las Vegas) is home to a glacier, the oldest living trees in the world (bristlecone pines), Nevada's second-highest peak (the majestic 13,000-foot Wheeler Peak), and the extensive Lehman Caves system, complete with stalagmites, stalactites, and rare shield formations. From Las Vegas, take US-93 North for 286 miles to NV-487 West for five miles to miles to NV-488 West for the final five miles.

Several Vegas-based tour companies offer full-day, round-trip excursions to Zion and Bryce Canyon National Parks. The professional guides at Adventure Photo Tours (702/889-8687 or 888/363-8687, Tues. and Thurs. 6am-8:30pm and by appointment, $239) take photographers and sightseers to both parks, serving a continental breakfast, lunch, bottled water, and snacks. Viator (Thurs. 6am-9pm, $239) offers a similar service, along with a three-day trip ($595) that includes trips to the Grand Canyon and Monument Valley.

Fremont Street Experience, and some of the more opulent hotels. The Hoover Dam tour ($65) can include a 15-minute helicopter flight over Lake Mead and the dam ($146) or a riverboat cruise on the lake ($100). To book a lake cruise directly, contact **Lake Mead Cruises** (866/292-9191, www.lakemeadcruises. com, adults $26, ages 3-11 $13, Sun. champagne brunch cruise adults $45, ages 3-11 $19.50, dinner cruise adults $61.50, ages 3-11 $25).

Vegas Tours (866/218-6877) has a full slate of outdoor, adventure, and other tours. Some of the more unusual ones include trail rides and full-day dude ranch tours ($120-$350) and a visit and tour of the Techatticup gold mine ($113-189). Tours of the Grand Canyon and other nearby state and national parks are available as well. **All Vegas Tours** (702/233-1627 or 800/566-5868) has all the usual tours: zip-lining (weight must be between 75 and 250 pounds, $159), tandem skydiving (age 18 and over, $239) and ATV sand-duning (valid driver's license required, $159). **Pink Jeep Tours** (702/895-6778 or 888/900-4480) takes visitors in rugged but cute and comfortable 10-passenger ATVs to such sites as Red Rock Canyon, Valley of Fire, and Hoover Dam.

There are plenty of other tour operators offering similar services. Search the Internet to find tours tailored for your needs, the best prices, and the most competent providers.

For history, nature, and entertainment buffs looking for a more focused adventure, themed tours are on the rise in Las Vegas. **Haunted Vegas Tours** (702/677-6499, most weekend nights 9:30pm, $85) takes an interesting if macabre trip to the "Motel of Death," where many pseudo-celebrities have met their untimely ends. Guides dressed as undertakers take you to the Redd Foxx haunted house, a creepy old bridge and an eerie park. The same company offers the **Las Vegas Mob Tour** (702/677-9015, $85), taking visitors to the sites of Mafia hits. Guides, dressed in black pin-striped suits and fedoras, tell tales of the 1970s, when Anthony "The Ant" Spilotro ran the city, and give the scoop on the fate of casino mogul Lefty Rosenthal. A pizza party is included in both tours.

JOIN OUR TRAVEL COMMUNITY
AND SIGN UP FOR OUR NEWSLETTER

MOON.COM

MAP SYMBOLS

▤	Expressway	○	City/Town	✈	Airport	⚓	Golf Course
	Primary Road	◉	State Capital	✈	Airfield	🅿	Parking Area
	Secondary Road	⊛	National Capital	▲	Mountain	▰	Archaeological Site
	Unpaved Road	★	Point of Interest	✛	Unique Natural Feature	⛪	Church
	Feature Trail	•	Accommodation		Waterfall	⛽	Gas Station
	Other Trail	▼	Restaurant/Bar	♠	Park		Glacier
	Ferry	■	Other Location				Mangrove
	Pedestrian Walkway			🚩	Trailhead		Reef
⊓⊓⊓⊓⊓	Stairs	▲	Campground	⛷	Skiing Area		Swamp

CONVERSION TABLES

°C = (°F - 32) / 1.8
°F = (°C x 1.8) + 32
inch = 2.54 centimeters (cm)
foot = 0.304 meters (m)
yard = 0.914 meters
mile = 1.6093 kilometers (km)
km = 0.6214 miles
fathom = 1.8288 m
chain = 20.1168 m
furlong = 201.168 m
acre = 0.4047 hectares
sq km = 100 hectares
sq mile = 2.59 square km
ounce = 28.35 grams
pound = 0.4536 kilograms
short ton = 0.90718 metric ton
short ton = 2,000 pounds
long ton = 1.016 metric tons
long ton = 2,240 pounds
metric ton = 1,000 kilograms
quart = 0.94635 liters
US gallon = 3.7854 liters
Imperial gallon = 4.5459 liters
nautical mile = 1.852 km

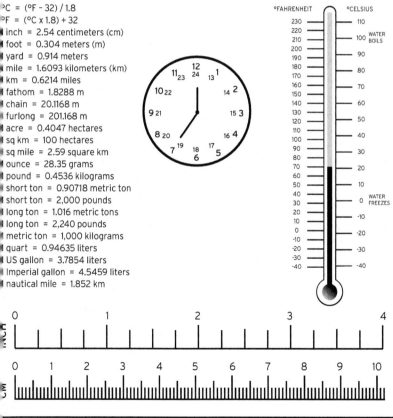

MOON SPOTLIGHT LAS VEGAS
Avalon Travel
a member of the Perseus Books Group
1700 Fourth Street
Berkeley, CA 94710, USA
www.moon.com

Editor: Kevin McLain
Copy Editor: Christopher Church
Graphics and Production Coordinator: Darren Alessi
Cover Design: Erin Seaward-Hiatt
Interior Design: Darren Alessi
Moon Logo: Tim McGrath
Map Editor: Albert Angulo
Cartographer: Brian Shotwell
Proofreader: Jamie Leigh Real

ISBN: 978-1-63121-295-6

31901056940333

CPSIA information can be obtained
at www.ICGtesting.com
Printed in the USA
LVOW02n1112150216
475146LV00008B/23/P